13.95

BANNED IN IRELAND

BANNED IN
IRELAND

CENSORSHIP & THE IRISH WRITER

Edited for Article 19 by

Julia Carlson

THE UNIVERSITY OF GEORGIA PRESS   ATHENS

© 1990 by Article 19
Introduction © 1990 by Julia Carlson.
The writers interviewed for this volume retain
copyright to their individual interviews.
Published by the University of Georgia Press
Athens, Georgia 30602
All rights reserved

Designed by Louise M. Jones
Set in Century Old Style

The paper in this book meets the guidelines for
permanence and durability of the Committee on
Production Guidelines for Book Longevity of the
Council on Library Resources.

Printed in the United States of America
94   93   92   91   90   5   4   3   2   1

Library of Congress Cataloging in Publication Data
Banned in Ireland : censorship and the Irish writer /
edited for Article 19 by Julia Carlson.
p. cm.
Includes bibliographical references.
ISBN 0-8203-1202-9 (alk. paper).
—ISBN 0-8203-1235-5 (pbk.)
1. English fiction—Irish authors—History and criticism.
2. English fiction— 20th century—History and criticism.
3. Fiction—Censorship—Ireland—History—20th
century.   4. Novelists, Irish—20th century—
Interviews.   5. Censorship—Ireland—History—
20th century.   6. Ireland—Intellectual life.
I. Carlson, Julia.   II. Article 19 (Organization)
PR8803.B36   1990
823'.914099415—dc20   89-27677   CIP

Benedict Kiely photo by Sean Larkin, Irish Press, Dublin;
John Broderick photo © Marion Boyars; John McGahern
photo © Michael Garvey; Edna O'Brien photo courtesy of
Edna O'Brien; Lee Dunne photo courtesy of *RTE Guide;*
Maurice Leitch photo © Tara Heinemann 1987; Brian Moore
photo © Herbert de Santane

Contents

Preface

Article 19, the International Centre on Censorship, is a human rights organization that campaigns on behalf of the right to freedom of expression worldwide. The organization, established in 1986, is independent of all governments and all political ideologies and religious beliefs. It takes its name from the nineteenth article of the Universal Declaration of Human Rights, 1948, which proclaims freedom of opinion and expression as an individual human right.

Article 19 has to date reported on freedom of expression and freedom of information in a range of countries. These studies have tended to give emphasis to the critique of legal principles and restrictions that formally determine the substance of these freedoms. The human dimension of censorship—its personal impact on writers, for instance—can be overlooked. *Banned in Ireland* gives voice to a group of novelists whose works have been banned in their own country, victims of an official literary censorship that permitted bureaucratic excess unchecked over decades by public opinion or the law. In compelling interviews conducted for Article 19 by Julia Carlson, seven leading Irish writers from North and South speak with feeling and with humour about their responses to having their fiction banned from circulation in Ireland by the state Censorship of Publications Board, in the company of such titles as *She Died Without Nylons* and *Hot Dames on Cold Slabs*.

The book reveals the less well understood side of Irish culture and community, a society that at least until the 1970s was in the grip of cultural isolationism, anti-intellectualism, and sexual repressiveness. Beyond the personal hurt and economic loss that being banned in Ireland has meant for the writers interviewed, and for many others, is the cautionary tale of a public that failed to come to their defence and that spurned their creative achievement.

Such protest as there was came from the literary community itself. In an appendix are assembled criticisms from some of the most illustrious names in Irish writing, who over the years spoke out about censorship, largely to no avail.

While no Irish writer is currently banned—the last, one of those interviewed in this volume, had his novel unbanned in 1988—the machinery of literary censorship is still in place. Article 19 hopes that this book and the painful and shameful experiences it relates will stimulate a public debate over the continued existence of a censorship tribunal in Ireland. It is difficult to reconcile the Censorship Board's role or its procedures with the country's constitutional and international commitments to freedom of expression or with Ireland's reputation abroad as a haven for culture.

Kevin Boyle[*]

May 1989

*Kevin Boyle is the founding director of Article 19 (1986–89). The current director is Frances D'Souza. Article 19's offices are located at 90 Borough High Street, London SE1 1LL, United Kingdom; telephone (01) 403 4822.

Introduction

Censorship of publications has been a fact of life in Southern Ireland for sixty years. Few major international authors have escaped the net of the Irish Censorship Board: to list all the books banned between 1929 and 1989 would be to list many of the major literary works of the twentieth century. For example Marcel Proust, William Faulkner, Ernest Hemingway, Saul Bellow, Vladimir Nabokov, Arthur Koestler, Heinrich Böll, Emile Zola, Jean Paul Sartre, Alberto Moravia, Sinclair Lewis, Dylan Thomas, Christina Stead, H. G. Wells, Mikhail Sholokov, Christopher Isherwood, Nadine Gordimer, and James Baldwin all have had their work banned. In particular, the Irish Censorship Board has made a target of Irish writers, systematically banning the work of several of them into the 1970s. From the banning of Liam O'Flaherty's *The House of Gold* in 1930 to the banning of Lee Dunne's *The Cabfather* in 1976, Irish readers have been denied access to work by the majority of Irish writers of fiction. Today the Censorship Board still exists. It has been nearly fifteen years since it has banned a book by an Irish writer, but writers from other countries continue to be its victims. In the past ten years, works by such internationally known figures as Roland Barthes, Susan Sontag, Monique Wittig, Anaïs Nin, Georges Bataille, Jerzy Kosinski, and Angela Carter have been banned.

The interviews and articles collected here have been assembled by Article 19 in order to expose the personal and intellectual impact that censorship has had on the lives and work of Irish writers. The story they tell is an alarming one of deprivation, harassment, and persecution, for censorship in Ireland has never been simply the banning of books: the paternalism that perpetuates Irish censorship succeeded for many years in blocking the interchange of ideas between Irish society and its writers.

In the wake of censorship, Irish writers have been deeply affected at a personal level. At the very least they have been hurt and enraged by the public and private humiliation they have suffered.

1

Some have seen their books burned and their families attacked. Others have lost their jobs and been forced to leave the country in order to earn a living. All have been tagged variously as nasty, indecent, and immoral.

Intellectually, the most serious consequence of censorship for Irish writers has been to undermine their influence in the community. Censorship has created a rift in Irish society, fostering the ignorance and provincialism of the Irish people and the intellectual and moral alienation of Irish writers. Many writers have left the country in anger and in search of greater intellectual freedom. Those who have remained have found themselves isolated and unable to give significant shape to Ireland's social, political, and cultural life.

In practice Irish writers are no longer personally threatened by censorship as they once were; however, the Censorship of Publications Board still operates, an indication that it has at least the tacit acceptance of the Irish people. The act is drawn upon today principally to ban pornography and information on abortion, but it is also applied arbitrarily. In 1987, for example, Alex Comfort's *The Joy of Sex,* published by Mitchell Beazley, was banned for the second time and Philip Rawson's *The Erotic Art of India,* published by Thames and Hudson, was also banned. An examination of the *Register of Prohibited Publications* for the past ten years suggests that books with a homosexual content have become a particular target of Irish censorship, with such titles as *The Gay World,* written by Dr. Martin Hoffman and published by Bantam, and *Male Homosexuals: Their Problems and Adaptations,* written by Martin S. Weinberg and Colin J. Williams and published by Penguin, being banned. As a moral issue, censorship continues to be a serious problem in Ireland today and a direct challenge to Article 19 of the United Nations Universal Declaration of Human Rights adopted in 1948: "Everyone has the right to freedom of opinion and expression; this right includes freedom to hold opinions without interference and to seek, receive and impart information and ideas through any media and regardless of frontiers."

The Censorship
of Publications Act

The fundamentals of censorship as it exists in Ireland today became law in 1929 with the enactment of the Censorship of Publications Act. Until this time the Obscene Publications Act, 1857, which still operates in Northern Ireland, and the Customs Consolidation Act, 1876 (section 42) were the two principal statutes in operation, and both had been inherited from British statute law. Under the British system there was no prior censorship; prosecution for obscenity in books was a matter for judge and jury. After the Irish Free State was established in 1922, British publishers were outside the jurisdiction of the Irish courts, and within Ireland a need was felt for a new censorship law that would more effectively control distribution of printed material, in particular the distribution of British newspapers and periodicals.[1]

Paradoxically, the reverse situation existed between Britain and Ireland with regard to censorship of the theatre. In Britain all plays were subject to prior scrutiny by the Lord Chamberlain before being performed, a practice that was abolished only in 1968. By contrast, the Theatres Act of 1843 did not apply in Ireland; consequently, the Irish theatre was not subject to prior censorship. There were notorious cases of unofficial censorship in the Irish theatre both before and after the establishment of the Irish Free State, including Cardinal Logue's campaign against W. B. Yeats's *The Countess Cathleen* in 1899, the riots at the Abbey Theatre when John Millington Synge's *The Playboy of the Western World* was first produced in 1907, and the closing of Tennessee Williams's *The Rose Tattoo* at the Pike Theatre in 1957.[2] Nevertheless, when the subject of censorship arose in Ireland in the 1920s, official censorship of the theatre was not debated and, as a result, never became a serious political issue in modern Ireland.

The Censorship of Publications Act, 1929, reflects the moral concerns and principles of the leaders of the new Irish Free State. In brief, the act provides for the banning of publications on three grounds: that they are "in . . . general tendency indecent or obscene" (part II, section 6); that they devote "an unduly large proportion of space to the publication of matter relating to crime" (part II, section 7); and that they advocate "the unnatural prevention of conception or the procurement of abortion or miscarriage" (part II, section 6). In a separate section, the word "indecent" is defined "as including suggestive of, or inciting to sexual immorality or unnatural vice or likely in any other similar way to corrupt or deprave" (part I, section 2).[3] In the wake of the Geneva Convention for the Suppression of the Circulation and Traffic in Obscene Publications of 1923, such moral legislation was not uncommon; in 1926, for example, a Judicial Proceedings (Regulation of Reports) Act was passed in Britain that restricted the reporting of divorce proceedings.[4]

What is most distinctive about the Irish Censorship of Publications Act is the way in which it provides for a Censorship Board of five members to assess publications. Appointed by the minister for justice, the members of the Censorship Board examine publications brought to their attention by customs officials or by members of the public. Although the Censorship Board is required to take into consideration, among other things, "the literary, artistic, scientific or historic merit or importance and the general tenor of the book" and "the class of reader . . . which may reasonably be expected to read such a book or edition" (part II, section 6), the board is answerable only to the minister for justice, not to a wider public. Similarly, the public at large is not entitled to know details of the activities or qualifications of members of the board. In effect, the Censorship Board has licence to operate in virtual secrecy. Once a publication is banned, its importation, sale, advertisement, and distribution are prohibited. Only the minister for justice can revoke a ban.

Since 1929, the Censorship of Publications Act has been liberalized twice. In the Censorship of Publications Act, 1946, provision was made for the minister for justice to appoint an Appeal Board of five members to whom authors, editors, publishers, and other named officials, specifically a group of any five members of the Irish Parliament, could apply in an effort to have publications unbanned. In theory this legislation liberalized the act considerably; in practice it had little effect because few appeals were lodged.

In 1967 further changes were made when the period for which a book could be banned as indecent or obscene was limited to twelve years with the provision that it could be rebanned if it was resubmitted to the Censorship Board. This legislation had an immediate impact when several thousand books automatically became unbanned in 1967. The scope of the act was weakened again when the Irish Parliament passed the Health (Family Planning) Act, 1979, which retained the prohibition on literature dealing with abortion but removed the Censorship Board's authority to ban books advocating "the unnatural prevention of conception."

Early Protest

Even before the Censorship of Publications Act, 1929, was made law, Ireland's writers began to protest against it. In the Senate, Oliver St. John Gogarty spoke vehemently against the introduction of literary censorship, although he did not contest restricting access to information on birth control.[5] The *Irish Statesman,* the major liberal journal of the period, which was edited by the writer AE (George Russell), published articles (three of them included here in the Appendix) denouncing censorship and its proponents. Writers from outside Ireland likewise took up the cause. In England, T. S. Eliot wrote on the dangers of censorship in his magazine, the *Criterion,* warning against "the tyranny of morality."[6] The American poet Ezra Pound, who was a close friend of W. B. Yeats, wrote admonitory letters to the *Irish Times* from his home in Italy, proclaiming that "the idiocy of humanity obviously knows no limits" and suggesting that "your voters might reflect on the effects of the American Censorship Law before sinking to the level of their perpetrators."[7]

The early protest against censorship by Ireland's writers is represented in this book in articles by W. B. Yeats, George Bernard Shaw, and AE. Their tone is one of warning as they predict the serious effect that passage of the act will have on the intellectual life of the nation. Like Pound, these three men were concerned about the principle of censorship; their immediate attention, however, was directed toward the wording of the proposed legislation. The definition of the word "indecent" as "calculated to incite sexual passion" was of particular concern. Shaw almost flippantly drew attention to the problem, asking, "By the way, what is to be done with the National Gallery under the Act?" Yeats pointed out that this definition, which was later modified, would deny the Irish people access to most of the world's religious and secular art: "The lawyers who drew up the Bill, and any member of the Dáil or Senate who thinks of voting for it, should study in some illustrated history of Art Titian's *Sacred and Profane Love,* and ask themselves if there is no one it could not incite to 'sexual passion,' and if they answer, as they are bound to, that there are many ask this further question of themselves. Are we prepared to exclude such art from Ireland and to sail in a ship of fools?"

Of equal concern to these writers was what was meant by the concept of public morality that was to be referred to several times in the legislation. AE argued at some length that the lack of precision in the wording of the act with regard to this concept would invite abuse because it would give the censors carte blanche to act for whatever they personally believed to be the public good:

> We confess we can form no precise idea of what is meant by the sentence which permits a book to be denounced if it "tends to inculcate principles contrary to public morality or is otherwise of such a character that the sale or distribution thereof is or tends to be injurious or detrimental to or subversive of public morality." A sentence like this is very vague. . . . There are people who think sincerely that socialistic literature is subversive of public morality. . . . Then again there are people who think sincerely that literature of agnosticism is subversive of public morality. . . . We have to be very precise in our definitions.

Behind the attention that Yeats, Shaw, and AE gave to the wording of the act lay their fear that its passage would seriously affect not only the intellectual life but the entire future of the nation. They were aware of the triumphalism that had infected Irish nationalists after the War of Independence and of the position of authority that the Irish Catholic church had assumed in the new state. They were aware that Ireland could easily become a nation of fanatics or, as Oliver St. John Gogarty put it, a country where "we should make use of our recently won liberty to fill every village and hamlet with little literary pimps" who would pride themselves on bringing books to the attention of the Censorship Board.[8]

Shaw was particularly articulate on the subject of Ireland's fate if the Censorship of Publications Act were to be passed and saw it as part of a more general effort on the part of the Free State to restrict and repress the freedom of the individual: "We shall never be easy until every Irish person is permanently manacled and fettered, gagged and curfewed, lest he should punch our heads or let out the truth about something." For him, Ireland was at a crucial point in its history, "in a position of special and extreme peril," and he ridiculed the notion that it could gain international respect by retreating from the modern world into a puritanical morality:

> In the nineteenth century all the world was concerned about Ireland. In the twentieth, nobody outside Ireland cares twopence what happens to her. . . . if, having broken England's grip of her, she slops back into the Atlantic as a little grass patch in which a few million moral cowards are not allowed to call their souls their own by a handful of morbid Catholics, mad with heresyphobia, unnaturally combining with a handful of Calvinists mad with sexphobia . . . then the world will let "these Irish" go their own way into insignificance without the smallest concern.

This early protest culminated in 1932 in the formation of the Irish Academy of Letters by Yeats and Shaw. In a letter to prospective academicians they wrote:

> There is in Ireland an official censorship possessing, and actively exercising, powers of suppression which may at any moment confine an Irish author to the British and American market, and thereby make it impossible for him to live by distinctive Irish literature.
>
> As our votes are counted by dozens instead of thousands and are therefore negligible, and as no election can ever turn on our grievances, our sole defence lies in the authority of our utterance. This, at least, is by no means negligible, for in Ireland there is still a deep respect for intellectual and

poetic quality. In so far as we represent that quality we can count on a consideration beyond all proportion to our numbers, but we cannot exercise our influence unless we have an organ through which we can address the public, or appeal collectively and unanimously to the Government.

We must therefore found an Academy of *Belles Lettres*. Will you give us your name as one of the founder members? [9]

There were nineteen founder members, G. Bernard Shaw, W. B. Yeats, AE, E. OE. Somerville, Padraic Colum, Lennox Robinson, Seumas O'Sullivan, T. C. Murray, St. John Ervine, Liam O'Flaherty, Forrest Reid, Brinsley MacNamara, Austin Clarke, F. R. Higgins, Oliver St. John Gogarty, Frank O'Connor, Peadar O'Donnell, Francis Stuart, and Sean O'Faolain, eight of whom were to have their work banned. Others, including Brinsley MacNamara, whose novel *The Valley of the Squinting Windows* was burned in his hometown, became victims of the unofficial censorship by which Irish writers were to be harassed for many years.

The Practice of Censorship

In spite of the fact that it was founded to protect Irish writers from censorship, the Irish Academy of Letters ultimately proved powerless in the face of its opposition. In the late twenties and early thirties the Irish Free State was a nation intent on purifying itself, and its people were deeply suspicious of artists and intellectuals. The writer Mervyn Wall recalled the suspicions of his father, who was an educated man and a barrister: "I remember well when my father opened the newspaper and here was Yeats giving out his famous speech—'No fool can call me friend.' My father just dismissed it. Everyone knew Yeats was mad. Shaw was mad. Anything to do with the arts was dangerous; that was the general feeling." [10]

The rhetoric by which the majority of people were swayed was that of Ireland's priests and politicians, who believed that by purging Ireland of all "indecencies" and foreign influences, they could shape it into a spiritual model for the world. Eamon de Valera, who came to power in 1932, saw Ireland as having a spiritual mission. The cultural isolationism that Shaw feared was, in effect, de Valera's ideal:

> That Ireland which we dreamed of would be the home of a people who valued material wealth only as a basis of right living, of a people who were satisfied with frugal comfort and devoted their leisure to the things of the spirit; a land whose countryside would be bright with cosy homesteads, whose fields and villages would be joyous with sounds of industry, the romping of sturdy children, the contests of athletic youths, the laughter of comely maidens; whose firesides would be the forums of the wisdom of serene old age.[11]

In practical terms this ideal was to be achieved by closing Ireland off from much of the modern world—everything from its fashions to its ideas. High on the list of evils were books and periodicals, both of which were regarded as potentially threatening to the racial purity of the state. The Council of Irish Bishops, Maynooth, warned in 1927: "The evil one is ever setting his snares for unwary feet. At the moment, his traps for the innocent are chiefly the dance hall, the bad book, the indecent paper, the motion picture, the immodest fashion in female dress—all of which tend to destroy the virtuous characteristics of our race."[12] Any mature and responsible discussion of sexuality was looked upon as sinful and seen to threaten the very moral fibre of the country. "The two words 'birth control' never appeared in a newspaper," Mervyn Wall recalled. "It was thought indecent even by the editor of a newspaper to mention those two words. We were all brought up to believe that there's only one sin and that has to do with sexual matters."

The moral fervour created by this obsession with national purity led to widespread public and private censorship even before the Censorship of Publications Act was introduced. Vigilantes took the burden of censorship upon themselves, seizing and burning the English Sunday newspapers, which were thought to be scandalous because of their coverage of divorce cases.[13] Books regarded as indecent were also burned—a practice that was to continue for many years, as Edna O'Brien reveals in her interview. Many middle-class people exercised a private censorship by destroying and defacing books in the privacy of their own homes. Mervyn Wall recalled:

> In my early twenties I had bought myself *Dubliners* and *Portrait of the Artist.* One day they disappeared from my book-

shelves in my bedroom. I have no doubt but that my father burnt them. . . . Years later I discovered that my father had torn out a couple of pages from Cervantes' *Don Quixote* because they described a bedroom scene, and that he had quite spoiled a fine edition of Chateaubriand by meticulously scoring out in ink throughout the set, every word he thought improper.[14]

In the name of decency, the nude form was covered almost wherever it was found. AE remembered the police denouncing "the engraving of a painting by Sir Frederick Leighton, who was spoken of by Watts as the purest and chastest painter of the nude," and recalled "attempts in Dundalk and Cork to prevent the poster of a nude baby reaching for soap being used as an advertisement." Those who were concerned about the fate of paintings in the National Gallery were not without reason. By 1930, all of the nudes had been removed from the Municipal Gallery, Dublin's principal gallery of modern art.[15]

When the Censorship of Publications Act became law, it legitimized this ongoing unofficial censorship. As there was no significant publishing of literature in Ireland, customs officials regularly detained books by Irish authors when they arrived in the country after publication abroad. Throughout Ireland Catholic activists, in particular members of the Catholic Truth Society, vetted books, underlining "indecent" passages and submitting books to the Censorship Board. Under pressure to read large numbers of books, the Censorship Board frequently recommended that books be banned on the basis of these passages, thereby breaching the requirement that a work be "in its general nature indecent or obscene."[16]

The puritanism and xenophobia apparent in unofficial censorship of the period were manifested equally in the decisions of the Censorship Board. Virtually any book that was brought to the attention of the Censorship Board and that contained a reference to sexual activity was banned. Novels by contemporary American, English, and Continental writers were banned in large numbers. Almost all contemporary Irish novelists had their work banned. The extremes to which the Censorship Board would go when it recommended the banning of work of an Irish nature became clear in 1941 with the

banning of Kate O'Brien's novel *The Land of Spices* and in 1942 with
the banning of *The Tailor and Ansty,* an anthropological work by an
English scientist, Eric Cross. *The Land of Spices* was banned for
one decorous sentence that alludes to an homosexual affair: "she
saw Etienne and her father, in the embrace of love."[17] *The Tailor
and Ansty,* an account of the lives of an elderly, uneducated rural
Irish couple based on interviews with Eric Cross, was banned because of its bawdy humour.[18] Significantly, this was not the only
anthropological work to be banned; Margaret Mead was a favourite
target of Irish censorship, with three of her studies being banned:
Growing up in New Guinea, Coming of Age in Samoa, and *Male and
Female.*

For Irish writers the most serious short-term effect of the Censorship of Publications Act was the increased unofficial censorship
that followed in its wake. Writers whose books were banned immediately became stigmatized and were regarded as legitimate
targets for harassment; however, virtually anyone who published
a book was suspect. Many writers whose books were not banned
suffered the same effects as those who had work censored. Mervyn
Wall recalled the way in which the Irish Catholic church put pressure on booksellers not to stock books that were critical of Irish
life: "I went in to Eason's, the big bookshop in O'Connell Street, on
one occasion, and the manager said to me, 'The theological censor
for the diocese called in here and in to the other bookshops, asking
them not to stock your book, but we don't allow ourselves to be
influenced by that.' Other small shops that sold a lot of Catholic
books would be influenced and then wouldn't stock it."[19]

Throughout the thirties, forties, and fifties, the moral fervour
that fuelled censorship so dominated Irish life that those who
objected to censorship risked being victimized if they protested
against it. Supplies in libraries and bookshops dwindled until the
books available to the Irish reader consisted of religious works
and those that celebrated Irish culture and Irish life. Virtually no
serious contemporary fiction was on the shelves.

Dermot Foley, who served as county librarian in Ennis, County
Clare, for many years and then became the first director of the
Library Council, recalled that librarians had little choice but to
remove books from library shelves when objections were raised;

the stock-in-trade of Irish libraries, particularly in rural areas, was "an Irish stew of imported westerns, sloppy romances, blood-and-murders bearing the *nihil obstat* of fifty-two vigilantes."[20] A good friend of the writer Frank O'Connor, Foley wrote to the *Irish Times* to protest the banning of O'Connor's *Kings, Lords and Commons* in 1961; Foley used a pseudonym, however, because he did not wish to jeopardize his job.[21] It was, he pointed out, a time of great fear, particularly in rural Ireland, when those who objected to censorship on moral grounds felt not only isolated but terrorized: "I was at a public meeting on censorship at Trinity College in 1987," Foley recalled, "and a young woman asked me why we had never protested against censorship. She was of a different generation; she would never understand." For over thirty years the unsullied society of which Irish priests and politicians had dreamed was realized: with few exceptions, Irish readers were kept in equal ignorance of sexual matters and of intellectual and artistic developments in their own country and abroad.

The Alienation of Irish Writers

Until 1946, when the Appeal Board was introduced, Irish writers had no recourse against censorship. They responded to their increasing persecution with increasing bitterness and alienation. Whereas writers of the twenties had been hopeful that they could influence public opinion, writers of the thirties became cynical about the effectiveness of protest against censorship in Ireland. Even Shaw, who repeatedly campaigned against censorship in England, was a case in point. When F. R. Higgins, then honorary secretary of the Irish Academy of Letters, asked Shaw to contest the legality of the 1933 banning of his *The Adventures of the Black Girl in Her Search for God* on the grounds of its illustrations, he refused. He sent a postcard in reply to the request, saying, "What's the use of flinging stones at the devil!"[22] Indeed, for many Irish writers censorship took on a comic dimension; they saw it as a black comedy and equated the very word "banned" with moral and artistic integrity.

The alienation of Irish writers is expressed most fully in two pieces included here, Liam O'Flaherty's "The Irish Censorship" and Samuel Beckett's "Censorship in the Saorstat." Deeply bitter, O'Flaherty and Beckett write out of disgust and disillusionment with Ireland in the thirties. They show a deep distrust of the Irish middle class and the Irish Catholic church, which they accuse of taking hold of the reins of power in the Irish Free State, and they reveal their belief that Ireland has become a country intent on repressing not only the "indecent or obscene" but intellectual exchange of any kind.

The contempt O'Flaherty and Beckett show for the leaders of the country is complete; they attack them for being dangerously ignorant, hypocritical, and self-serving. Beckett repeatedly mocks the ignorance of the politicians who debated the Censorship of Publications Bill, turning their own words against them: "The stock allusion to the *Decameron* caused no little flutter in the Senate, but was skilfully negotiated by Senator Johnson: 'I do not think it has any great reputation as a book.'" O'Flaherty argues that the church and the middle class use censorship to foster the ignorance of the poor and to preserve their own authority: "The tyranny of the Irish Church and its associate parasites, the upstart Irish bourgeoisie . . . maintains itself by the culture of dung, superstition and ignoble poverty among the masses."

The principal effect of censorship, O'Flaherty and Beckett argue, has been to turn Ireland into an intellectual and moral wasteland. It has become a country where repression and ignorance are celebrated, where moral values have become so twisted that, in the imagery used by both writers, a living hell has been mistaken for paradise. O'Flaherty identifies with ordinary citizens as victims of an attempt to destroy the interchange of ideas: "the censorship of literature was imposed, lest men like me could teach the Irish masses that contact with dung is demoralizing, that ignorance is ignoble and that poverty, instead of being a passport to Heaven, makes this pretty earth a monotonous Hell." Beckett focuses on the combined effects of the censorship of literature and information on birth control. For him, Ireland is grotesque—a bleak, perverted paradise: "Sterilization of the mind and apotheosis of the litter suit well together. Paradise peopled with virgins and the earth with decorticated multiparas."

The Voice of Reason

In the 1940s the novelists Sean O'Faolain and Frank O'Connor rose to prominence in the protest against censorship. They made their presence felt in constant letters to newspapers and initiated a correspondence in the *Irish Times* in 1942 that led to the first major Senate debate on censorship since the passage of the act in 1929.[23] Together, they were responsible for creating a climate of moral and civic awareness in Ireland that led to the formation of the Appeal Board in 1946.

Throughout the first half of the decade O'Faolain's chief organ of protest was the *Bell,* the journal he founded and edited from 1940 to 1946. The only liberal journal of the period in Ireland, it was a compendium of literature and social commentary in which, in monthly editorials, O'Faolain took on the monumental task of exploring the state of the nation and waged a rigorous campaign not only against censorship but also against the cultural deprivation and antiintellectualism of Irish life.

In theory and in principle O'Faolain was not wholly opposed to censorship; however, he objected strongly to the wholesale official and unofficial censorship practiced in Ireland and addressed the problem in several editorials. In "Our Nasty Novelists," for example, he attacked those who wished Irish writers to provide an idealized image of Irish life and praised the country's realistic novelists, virtually all of whom had their fiction banned, for their sanity: "the only real sanity in this island, as far as culture is concerned, is in the novels of our Realists."[24]

What made O'Faolain's editorials particularly effective was the way in which he integrated his attack on censorship with a multifaceted analysis of Irish cultural life. The editorial included here, "The Mart of Ideas," offers a typical example of O'Faolain's technique, as he warns that censorship is at the root of a larger cultural malaise. He argues that public discussion of controversial issues, especially those that challenge the teaching of the Catholic church or threaten the nationalist ideals of the Gaelic League, is nonexistent in Ireland. Moreover, he goes further to argue that censorship is essentially fascist, that it has created a dangerous and widespread intellectual indifference in Ireland that seriously endangers the conscience of every individual and leaves the country open to those who would impose a rigid orthodoxy: "It is against . . . every man who takes life seriously, who takes thought seriously, who takes art and culture seriously, that the Literary Censorship is directed by those who would establish in place of thought a rigid orthodoxy that no man must even discuss, let alone question or deny."

Unlike O'Faolain, O'Connor never conducted a systematic protest against censorship. In his thinking he was more radical than O'Faolain, however, and challenged him in the *Bell* for not taking a stronger stand against the principle of censorship.[25] For many years, O'Connor himself was one of the major targets of official and unofficial censorship in Ireland. Not only were his books banned; he was effectively blacklisted from employment. In 1943 he was given a weekly newspaper column in the *Sunday Independent,* which he wrote under the pseudonym of Ben Mayo; according to Dermot Foley, O'Connor's position remained so vulnerable that he did not even tell close friends that it was he who wrote the column.[26]

In the article included here O'Connor provides a retrospective on three decades of Irish censorship. The article is the text from O'Connor's side of a 1962 debate at the College Historical Society of Trinity College where he and Justice Kevin Haugh, who was then chairman of the Appeal Board, spoke on opposing sides to the motion that "Irish censorship is insulting to Irish intelligence." At this time books by Irish writers were still being banned in large numbers, as the interviews that follow reveal; an anticensorship protest had begun to make itself felt, however, and as a result censorship had become a subject for debate in Irish universities.

It is a measure of the changing climate of opinion that O'Connor's speech is witty and anecdotal rather than bitter and castigating and that he won the debate by an overwhelming majority of forty to nine. In spite of his lightness of tone, O'Connor makes it clear that he believes censorship to be a serious threat in Ireland in the 1960s. He sees the means by which censorship is imposed as particularly insidious, deploring the fact that it is not a matter for the courts of law: "I don't want to depend for protection on any individual, whatever his taste and judgment. As a citizen of this country I want to depend for protection on the constitution and the courts." To O'Connor, as to many other writers, the most serious long-term effect of censorship is the way it has sapped the cultural life of the country, fostering anti-intellectualism and keeping the Irish people in a continuing state of ignorance about artistic and intellectual developments in their own country: "to me the most awful thing about the censorship is the way it perpetuates the negative attitude we oppose to every manifestation of intellect and scholarship. . . . We have a great literature, published by Englishmen and Americans, and, thanks to our censors, ninety-nine per cent of it is out of print and unobtainable, so that . . . we have brought up a generation which knows nothing of its own country, or its own literature."

A Silent Vigil

The tradition of active protest against censorship that began with Yeats, AE, and Shaw ended, effectively, with O'Connor and O'Faolain. The next generation of writers to have their work banned looked upon censorship as an anachronism; they were to become so disillusioned with the political process in Ireland that, with few exceptions, they removed themselves from public affairs as a matter of principle. For them, Irish society was not malleable but monolithic, and inaction became, in effect, a moral stance.

The interviews that follow are the legacy of this inaction and give voice to the continuing protest against censorship of seven of these writers, creating a dialogue between them and writers of earlier generations. In these interviews Benedict Kiely, John Broderick, John McGahern, Edna O'Brien, Lee Dunne, Maurice Leitch, and Brian Moore discuss the reasons for the development of Irish censorship, their personal experiences of official and unofficial censorship, their experience of living and working within the Irish literary community or their reasons for having left that community to go into exile, their attitudes toward censorship in Ireland today, and their views on censorship as a matter of principle.

While the topics they cover are similar, each writer brings an individual perspective and insight to Irish censorship. Benedict Kiely, the only one of these writers to have lived in Dublin through the forties and fifties, remembers the impact of official and unofficial censorship upon his own life and upon Dublin literary life of the period. John Broderick describes how censorship operated in the provincial town of Athlone where he was reared, recalling how oppressive such towns were for the writer and providing insight into the sexual puritanism that created in many Irish people a pathological attitude toward homosexuality.

The most controversial writers of the 1960s in Ireland, John McGahern and Edna O'Brien, document the brutality that censorship unleashed on individual writers. John McGahern recalls how he lost his job as a primary school teacher in 1965 after the banning of his second novel, *The Dark,* and identifies the writer as "one of the only uncompromised moral authorities" in Irish society. Edna O'Brien analyzes the expectations and restrictions that exist for women in Ireland as she describes the persecution she suffered as a result of the banning of her books and reveals the barricades that Irish society sets before women who wish to break away from traditional gender roles.

In the 1970s Lee Dunne became the principal target of Irish censorship. Reared in working-class Dublin, he focuses in particular upon the socioeconomic implications of censorship.

The perspective of writers from Northern Ireland is provided by Maurice Leitch and Brian Moore. Maurice Leitch looks at Irish censorship from the point of view of the Northern Protestant, revealing his estrangement from the literary tradition of the Irish Republic and his conviction that there is little difference between the repressive ideologies of Northern and Southern Ireland. Brian Moore looks back on Ireland as an expatriate, recalling how censorship blighted his literary education and made him realize that his alienation from Irish society was complete.

Together the testimonies of these writers create a portrait of the effects of censorship on Irish society. Like the writers of previous generations, the seven writers interviewed here are deeply critical of the society that gave rise to and perpetuated censorship, identifying it with the isolationism and xenophobia of Irish nationalism, the puritanism and authoritarianism of the Irish Catholic church, and the striving for respectability of the Irish middle classes. In particular, they focus on the destructive impact of sexual repression on Irish society—at a psychological level for individuals and at a cultural and intellectual level for the society at large—at times making a distinct connection between the anti-Englishness of the Irish Free State and sexual repression in Ireland. They criticize Irish society for its intolerance, its ignorance of and arrogance toward human rights, and its antiintellectual ethos, all of which they see as persisting today, particularly in the actions of anti-abortion groups. Although they differ in their attitudes toward the banning of pornography, these writers are in agreement in their attitude toward censorship as a matter of principle, regarding it as self-defeating and a serious moral threat to human rights.

Today none of these writers is banned in Ireland. The last book by an Irish writer to be banned, Lee Dunne's *The Cabfather*, was released in 1988. Even though censorship is practiced less frequently than in the past, it must be considered a continuing threat in Ireland today. The Censorship of Publications Act is still in place and serious literature continues to be banned in Ireland as in no other country in Western Europe. The moral ethos that gave rise to Irish censorship persists. As recently as 1988, Ireland's Supreme Court upheld a ban on family-planning clinics' providing information on abortion facilities in Britain.[27] A censorship mentality exists in Ireland. As long as the present censorship law remains in place, freedom of information and artistic freedom are in jeopardy.

INTERVIEWS

BENEDICT KIELY

Benedict Kiely was born near Dromore, County Tyrone, in 1919. In 1940 he moved to Dublin, where he studied at University College, Dublin, and later worked as a journalist. In the 1940s and 1950s, he had three novels banned by the Irish Censorship Board: *In a Harbour Green* (1949), *Honey Seems Bitter* (1952), and *There Was an Ancient House* (1955). A popular broadcaster and raconteur, he has been at the centre of Dublin literary life for over forty years. His recent works include the novel *Nothing Happens in Carmincross* (1985) and *A Letter to Peachtree* (1987), a collection of short stories. He was interviewed in Dublin by Julia Carlson for Article 19 on 15 April 1987.

The Personal Experience
of Censorship

**You would have been ten years old when the first Censor-
ship Act was passed in 1929. How conscious were you of
censorship when you were growing up?**

Not growing up, you wouldn't have been so much up in the North.
Wait till we see when it would have first occurred to one. It would
have to be almost in my Dublin days—from about 1940 onwards.
The banning of Kate O'Brien's *The Land of Spices:* that was the
first censorship ban that I think I was conscious of and conscious of
it as a complete and teetotal outrage. That line and a half when the
nun as a young girl discovers that her father was having, you know
the thing, just a line and a half, and under this "in general indecent
or obscene" the entire book was banned. That would have been my
first awareness, I think, the banning of *The Land of Spices.*

**When you moved to Dublin and started to write fiction, how
conscious were you of the spectre of censorship hanging over
you then?**

You became immediately conscious then. O'Flaherty, O'Faolain,
and O'Connor, of course. O'Flaherty perhaps first because I think
he would have been banned before any of them. Then O'Faolain's
first collection of stories was banned, *Midsummer Night Madness.*
Then after that it just went from bad to worse. They were banning
everything. In fact, by the time I got around to the distinction,
you'd be damned nearly ashamed if you weren't banned. You were
annoyed in one way, but you also felt you had joined the elect. I can
only think of two Irish writers, that would be Michael McLaverty
—there was nothing they could catch on to banning Michael—that
was not his world—and Francis MacManus, that just escaped the
censorship. Francis was a solid citizen by that time. But when he
wrote *The Fire in the Dust,* I think if the censorship had known

what it was about—it was about censorship, in fact, in a curious way—that they would have banned that. But everybody else was. No, Peadar O'Donnell never was.

Mervyn Wall wasn't.

Mervyn came very close to it. There was a bit of a flurry about the Fursey books, but, no, Mervyn was never banned. Anyhow, mostly what they went for was something relating to sex, and, God knows, it was very mild sex, too. I'm sure you could have put in every heresy from Albigensianism fore and aft and ten times over, and nobody would notice the difference.

Was it just sex? Or was it also that Irish people were being shown in a bad light?

It was just sex. Well, Professor Magennis who was chairman of the Censorship Board did once make a remark about O'Connor and O'Faolain that they couldn't write novels; all that they did was to write short stories and pad it out with smut for the English market. The assumption being that the English read nothing but smut, I suppose: they wouldn't buy a book unless it was smutty.

There was a lot of anti-English feeling behind the censorship, wasn't there?

The thing came in in a very curious way in keeping out foreign periodicals and all that. That was definitely just an anti-English thing. And it came in at a very bad period when the country was spun out with Civil War in the 1920s. I'm told there is a legend that it came in by accident after Kevin O'Higgins, the minister for justice, was murdered, that his successor, a man by the name of Fitzgerald-Kenney, was rooting around in his office one day and found this bill which O'Higgins had drafted but had pigeonholed. He thought he would shut the mouths of these puritans or whatever by drafting the bill; then he would pigeonhole and forget about it. But Fitzgerald-Kenney came upon it, and to keep himself occupied and to look like being a minister of something, he brought it in—at least, the bill finally ended up as an act anyway. Some of his speeches—you have to look them up in the Government publications of the time —I believe, were quite hilarious. You know that of course censors would not have to go to the trouble of really reading all of a book like *Ulysses* or things like that.[1]

Was that how the censorship actually operated—by the marked passages system?

The Catholic Truth Society had a group of people reading books and marking passages in them, and they would send them in to the censorship. I remember the late Seamus Brady, a journalist and a great journalist, saying to me an extraordinary thing. He said, "A neighbour of mine has a house full of new books, dust covers and all." I said, "Does he review books for maybe the English papers?" "Not at all," he said. "He gets them from the Catholic Truth Society to mark the dirty passages. I never knew the man could even read." But there he was reading the books, looking for the dirty bits and sending them in. And that was how the thing actually worked.

Would you say, then, that Irish censorship was also an arm of the Catholic church?

It was, I suppose, the climate created by the Catholic church that made it possible. On the other hand you had many liberal priests— liberal is perhaps not the right word—many sensible priests who objected to it and thought the whole thing was nonsense, too. But quite clearly, it could not have come into existence, I would say, except for that certain ambiance of the Catholic church as it was. It originally came from a group of, I suspect, puritanical, fervent nationalists keeping out filthy, foreign publications. Strongly puritan Catholicism originally made the thing possible. There would be no way that you could say the church wasn't responsible.

Eilis Dillon has written that she longed to write a book that would be banned.[2] Did most people feel that way?

There was that feeling. There was also a certain comic aspect of it.

And what was that?

It just got funny. You see, if they were banning everything, the thing was just going ultimately to laugh itself out of existence, which it damn nearly did until de Valera took the definite Irish solution, or a de Valera solution, to an Irish problem anyway, putting in the Appeal Board. Then it became utterly comic because a book was no sooner banned than if you appealed it would be unbanned.

Did you or your publisher ever make an appeal?

I never did willingly. My first banning was Cape and that was *In a Harbour Green. Honey Seems Bitter* was banned. That was Methuen. Methuen asked me at the time and so did Cape, and I said not to bother to appeal. That to appeal was to admit that they had any legal right or constitutional right to ban, which I always maintained and O'Faolain did too. You'd have to take them to court to challenge the constitutionality of it, and legal costs and all that sort of thing would leave you up the creek. So nobody ever did it, anybody that I know of.

***There Was an Ancient House* was unbanned though, wasn't it? How did that happen?**

This was just so goddamned outrageous. It was as near as I could get to writing, heaven help the remark and put it in quotations, "a religious book." This was banned. And a very strange thing—I think it was Tom Kilroy's inaugural at the English Literature Society at University College, Dublin. Jerry Hogan, the professor of English, was there that night and I was there that night. I was just back from Germany. I'd been there on a press job. In fact, I was in Hamburg when I heard that the book was banned. Pan Collins rang me. Jerry was on the Appeal Board, and he said, "We unbanned your book. It should never have been banned anyway." But another member of the Appeal Board met me one day in the street. He was a bluff, forward man; he's dead now. "I voted against the unbanning of your book," he said. He knew that I had been talking to Jerry, and he rather foolishly thought that Jerry would be so indiscreet

as to mention names to me, which of course he wouldn't. But I
said, "Why in God's name?" "Oh," he said, "that incident of the
girl getting in nude into the lake was incongruous." "But," I said,
"look, you're not on an Appeal Board to teach me how to write
novels. You're supposed to be interpreting so-called law 'in general
tendency indecent or obscene.'" And he turned and walked away
from me and didn't speak to me for several years afterwards. Not
too long before he died I'm glad to say we spoke again. That sort
of crazy attitude.

**You mentioned the problem of money in connection with the
Appeal Board. How were you affected financially by the banning of your books?**

That was the real nasty aspect of it—that you actually lost money
on it, for what your sales in Ireland, so to speak, considering the
population, would be worth anyway. But you lost a large proportion
of those since the Catholic bookshops would not touch you. If you
had the name for being censored, they wouldn't order your next
book in case they'd be left holding the stock. I know that a lady
went into this bookshop in Dublin—this is extraordinary—looking
for my novel *Dogs Enjoy the Morning* [1968]. By this time I'd long
ceased being banned, and he had the novel all right, but he had it
under the counter. He wouldn't display it because I had the name
for being a banned author.

**So it snowballed then, and books of yours that weren't offi-
cially banned were concealed or never ordered.**

Of course, because you had the name for being banned. I suspect
they stopped banning me at that time because I'd been so long in
the *Irish Press* that they must have thought I was first cousin to de
Valera or something like that, so I became respectable by being on
the *Irish Press*. [3]

**Do you think your working on the *Irish Press* had that effect,
that the decision to stop banning your books was a political
decision so to speak?**

I think ultimately it would have. I was literary editor there for about fourteen years, and you couldn't be literary editor of de Valera's paper and be an "indecent or obscene" person. Quite obviously. So that might have had some effect.

You mentioned unofficial censorship by booksellers. Did you ever have any difficulty getting books you wished to read?

I was on the newspapers and books were always around, so you could get them. I never had any problems. I took Henry Miller back with me from Paris. You just threw them in your briefcase, and nobody bothered that I ever noticed. When I was doing *Modern Irish Fiction* [1950], I wanted to reread O'Faolain's *Midsummer Night Madness.* I hadn't a copy of it; I just read it in the National Library. They had the books there in a special section. You just filled in the docket, and you wanted to read it for research purposes, and that was that. No question at all about it.

Were you or anyone else you know subjected to unofficial censorship of any other kind? You once wrote about Brinsley MacNamara being harassed after he wrote *The Valley of the Squinting Windows.*[4]

I know a lot about *The Valley of the Squinting Windows* because Brinsley MacNamara and I were very close. What actually happened was that everybody in his hometown of Delvin thought that they were in the book or at least some did. I have been in Delvin quite often with Brinsley, and there were houses into which he could go and was welcome and other houses into which he could not enter. It became a village quarrel, and his father was actually assaulted. His father was the schoolmaster at Ballinvalley beyond Delvin. A man at Collinstown Cross on the far side of Delvin told me it used to be great amusement to cycle in on a Saturday evening into Delvin to see them fighting up and down the street about *The Valley of the Squinting Windows.* A local butcher burned the book, and an old lady went into the house and said, "Thank God, the trouble's over now. The book's burned." I think that's a lovely medieval attitude. That's absolutely true.

What about you personally? I know there was some controversy when you left the *Irish Independent* newspaper. Did what happened there have anything to do with the banning of your books?

What happened in the *Irish Independent* was that—believe it or not, I was in the leader writers' room there, and I was, you might say, practically their authority on Catholic affairs, but not quite as bad as that or as good as that. I had been a year or something in the Jesuit novitiate, and I had worked on the weekly Catholic newspaper, the *Standard,* with Peter O'Curry. Whether that qualified you as a theologian or not, I am not quite certain, but if they had any query of that sort that couldn't be solved in the newsroom, and most of them were solved there, they'd bring it in to me. The editor at that time was a very good man, Frank Geary, but he was a terribly conservative man. I was doing theatre for them, too, and I had reviewed Farquhar's *The Recruiting Officer* and gave it a tremendous review, praised the language to the clouds and all that. Poor Frank Geary was smothered with letters from complaining readers who went to the Gate Theatre on the strength of the play being recommended in the *Irish Independent* and had to run from all the bad language.

Oliver Weldon, Brinsley MacNamara's son, was then assistant editor, I think, of the *Evening Herald,* and at a board meeting at which Oliver was deputizing for the then editor of the *Evening Herald,* the then manager, I won't bother mentioning his name, wanted me fired because of this dirty book [*In a Harbour Green*]. Frank Geary said he objected to the book and all that, but there was no question what I did with my own time was my own business. I did my job for him, and that was all he was concerned with. I wouldn't have known that only for Oliver Weldon, who told me about it. I discussed the matter at that time then and asked Frank Geary about it. I said flat, "Did the banning of the book embarrass you?" And he said, "To tell you the truth, it did now. It did a bit." Then he mentioned the business about *The Recruiting Officer.* He told me then that he wouldn't stop me going to plays, but if I thought that there was anything awkward about a play would I tell him before I wrote a note.

I think the last one I did was *Volpone*. Donald Wolfit was doing *Volpone* in the Gaiety, and at the attempted rape scene a stern-looking father got up and herded his two daughters out of the theatre. It's amazing. People wouldn't do it nowadays. You just wouldn't believe it. People were innocent and naive. That's the only way you can consider it. So I mentioned this to Frank Geary and he laughed merrily. He said, "Well, at the request of the editor of the *Irish Independent,* you are going to compress Ben Jonson into a short review." Which I merrily did. I'd already given my notice to the *Irish Independent.* I had mentioned the matter to R. M. Smiley of the *Irish Times* and M. J. MacManus. M.J. was then literary editor of the *Irish Press,* a very great man. They both immediately offered me jobs, and they sort of cast lots for the corpse, but M.J. could offer me more money and Smiley agreed.

So you resigned. Or were you fired?

No. I gave my notice. No, I wasn't fired. I gave my notice and left in the normal way.

But it was the banning of the book?

Well, it was. You see, the question of being stopped doing theatre did rather annoy one. After that I got a rather snooty review—I knew who did it, too—about *Honey Seems Bitter* when it came out. The heading on the review was simply "A Nasty Novel." That was the heading. If you did want to sell a few copies of a book, there are enough people in Ireland that would rush quickly to buy it if they saw "A Nasty Novel."

The Irish Literary Community

You lived in Dublin when censorship was at its worst in the forties and fifties. Were you aware of censorship creating a sense of community among Irish writers?

I don't think it did, no. They regarded the thing, most of them, rather lightly. Nobody apart from Brendan Behan when he was half

jarred was going to take the thing seriously. My favourite censorship story which I must tell you was about Brendan. Brendan, when
Borstal Boy was banned [in 1958], came in to me one evening in
the *Irish Press,* and his chief indignation was that a lot of country
cawboges [yokels], sitting up in a room in Merrion Square, had the
effrontery to ban his book in his town. That was the basis of it. We
went over to Gerry Dwyer's pub to meet the late Philip Rooney,
the writer; Brendan was still giving out blazes about censorship.
This man came up to me; his Northern accent was even worse than
my own. He said, "What's he complaining about?" I explained that
he had a book banned by the censorship, et cetera, et cetera. And
he says to Brendan, myself, and Philip, "What size is the book?"
"What do you mean what size is it?" "I asked you a question. What
size is the book?" Brendan gave him a rough idea of the cubic content of *Borstal Boy.* He thought for a moment and said, "I could run
you over two thousand copies." He was a butter smuggler, and he
was estimating how many copies would fit into his truck crossing
the border. He could do it in his head. That's absolutely true. That
was actually said.

**Why do you think many Irish writers accepted the presence
of censorship even when they disapproved of it?**

I suppose they felt like myself—that you just went on and did your
writing and forgot about it. Maybe it was a wrong attitude—I don't
know—but I never saw anybody getting worked up about it much. I
don't ever remember being particularly aggrieved at being banned.
You merely lost a bit of money, but so what. It wasn't that much
money anyway. And as I said, you did have the feeling that you
were with the right people because everybody else was banned
that was any damned good, well, with those few exceptions.

**What about Sean O'Faolain? Did he provide a kind of a focus
for the literary community?**

O'Faolain was the man that spoke out against censorship continually. He wasn't wild about it or anything; he spoke rationally about
the nonsense of the thing. I read recently that O'Faolain was suffering from frustration and all that under the de Valera regime, which

isn't at all, I don't think, exact by any means. O'Faolain never suffered from frustration at all. He loved the fight, I think. He was a monument in that he stayed. He was a good deal out of the country, but he was still permanently and, you might say, visibly and audibly here all the time and in that way was, I think, a tremendous influence on everybody who came after him.

So much has been said about Ireland driving its writers into exile.

> This lovely land that always sent
> Her writers and artists to banishment
> And in a spirit of Irish fun
> Betrayed her own leaders, one by one.
> —*James Joyce, "Gas from a Burner"*

It is true that writers have gone into exile. Joyce did it out of, I think, a proper pride. He wanted that isolation and detachment. Padraic Colum told me that when he went to the U.S.A., if he could have found a job in Dublin worth a pound a week, he would have stayed, but he couldn't. Material reasons drove him out, as it drove other people out, too. Francis Hackett went in indignation when his novel [*The Green Lion*] was banned by the censorship. AE left because of the Black and Tan War, Civil War, and all that.

What about your choice to stay?

Whether I chose or not I don't know. It just so happened that way. I was never a wild man for making choices of that sort. Materially, I was OK, you see. I was working on the papers and that was all right with me, so I never really felt like moving on to London. One thing that, I suppose, kept one at least until the war was over, as the historian Kevin B. Nowlan once said to me—we were walking around once during the war years, and Kevin must have been beginning to feel the constrictions of neutrality—he said, "If we ran away to sea, we couldn't get beyond the three-mile limit." The thought of Kevin and myself running away to sea is definitely something to laugh at.

Ireland Today

What do you think of Ireland as a place for the writer today?

The first simple disadvantage is material. The small population, I mean, that's the basic fact. But the writer, generally, is fairly well regarded, I think, by the Irish people.

You wrote in an article entitled "The Whores on the Half-Doors" that the writer was looked upon as an object of suspicion and contempt in Ireland.[5] Do you still think that's true?

I don't know did I say 'contempt'?

Yes.

My goodness. Maybe there might be that element somewhere. Suspicion, yes, because of this problem about putting people into books, that there's this jackass of a fellow in the corner watching everybody, taking notes. I was explaining to the filmmaker David Shaw-Smith's right-hand man about using the word "freelance" and said, "In any other country in the world, freelance is respectable. It means you're a man standing up on your own two feet, but in Ireland the assumption would be that—ah, sure, the poor fellow, he couldn't get a job, or even if he got a job, he couldn't keep it with the drink. That's why he's a freelance." There is that sort of withering Irish attitude to a whole lot of things. How much of it is actually serious I'm never quite sure.

Things have changed a great deal for writers in Ireland.

They most certainly have. There are bursaries and tax-free and all that.[6] There's no question or doubt about it that things are vastly improved for young writers compared with what they were in the forties. What you would miss would be a good supply of good periodicals. We don't have that; printing costs. But then David Marcus did magnificent work in the *Irish Press,* publishing young writers.

Definitely material things are better for young writers now. The only honour you got in the old days was to be called "indecent or obscene." I suppose it was the only laurel wreath that Ireland was offering to writers in that particular period.

The Censorship Board still exists. Do you think it's a threat today?

It easily could be. The amount of trash that's floating around and that the kids are being subjected to, of course, gives them a sort of argument.

Do you think that a censorship mentality exists in Ireland today?

You've had that recently in these referendums and all that.[7] You always get these weird pressure groups, and they can actually appear quite sinister at times. Some of them get into a frenzy about abortion and the like. You've seen that happen and it's just the same mentality.

The Principle of Censorship

Do you believe in censorship as a matter of principle?

As a matter of principle, that censorship should most certainly never have existed. It was completely nonsensical. It had no reason. Generally, I would say there is no instance in history, I think, of a successful censorship having done what it set out to do. It only makes things worse, even from the point of view of the censors. The repression leads to even worse results.

In what sort of way?

For instance, suppose somebody's running around looking for banned books. God bless us, even that is a sort of moral step downwards, when you're hunting around looking for something because you think there might be something obscene in it that you would like to read. All forms of repression just bring out the worst in people, I think, ultimately.

Can you see any instances in which you would be in favour of censorship?

No, I can't.

You once wrote that you believed censorship is rooted in fear.[8] Do you still believe that?

There is that blunt refusal to face up to what is going on in the world and actually thinking that you can shelter young people from all these things. You can't do it, not in the world we're living in today. You never could do it, I suppose, at any time, except you wanted them to live like Amish people, and even the Amish people break out now and again and clear off. The fear. There is a basis of fear in it, of course.

JOHN BRODERICK

John Broderick was born in 1927 in Athlone, County West-meath, where his family owned a large bakery. His first novel, *The Pilgrimage*, was banned by the Irish Censorship Board in 1961. *The Pilgrimage* was highly critical of the bourgeoisie of provincial Ireland and exceptional in Irish fiction of that period for its treatment of homosexuality. His other fiction includes *The Trial of Father Dillingham* (1981), *The Rose Tree* (1985), and *The Flood* (1987). In 1981 Broderick moved to England; he was interviewed by Julia Carlson for Article 19 in Bath on 23 June 1987. He died in England in 1989.

The Personal Experience
of Censorship

Your work is seen as more within the European Catholic tradition than the narrow Irish one. Do you think Irish censorship is the product of a distorted notion of spiritual morality?

I think it's not easy to separate Ireland, even the Ireland in which I was brought up, from the general European civilization because the church had such an influence in Ireland through its educational facilities both for boys and girls, and that was originally influenced by Europe. But, of course, Irish Catholicism after the treaty had a tremendous feeling of triumphalism. The great peak of that was the Eucharistic Congress in 1932, and the church, after playing second fiddle to the British government for so many centuries, suddenly became a chief influence on the people.[1]

Would you see Irish censorship as an arm of the Irish Catholic church?

Yes. Not one hundred percent. The people in power in Ireland in the twenties and thirties were very narrow-minded, and I think they got the church they wanted.

Narrow-minded in what kind of way?

Narrow-minded sexually. They weren't intellectually narrow-minded. You could publish a book attacking the church through Thomist philosophy or through the philosophy of Jean-Paul Sartre, something like that. It would not be banned. It wasn't intellectually biased, but it was very biased as regards sex, which was the *verboten,* forbidden thing in Ireland when I was growing up.

When you were growing up, what exactly did censorship mean?

It meant that you had written something that was very sexy. That was what it meant fundamentally. It wasn't very true, but then their idea was very narrow. Kate O'Brien's *The Land of Spices* was banned for just one phrase; you know the one. Ridiculous. They banned *The Razor's Edge* by Somerset Maugham and quite a lot of Graham Greene, all kinds of stupid things like that. There used to be a list of banned books in the paper, and a book like one of Kate O'Brien's books would be in a list which included titles like *Hot Dames on Cold Slabs*. I always remember that title. It's a great one. They overplayed their hand because they were ignorant people. There was a period during which "banned in Ireland" meant something, but after a while it meant about as much as "banned in Boston."

When you began to write, how conscious were you that your work might be banned?

I wrote my first book as I wanted to write it and as it came to me. The Censorship Board did not enter my mind then or thereafter. I only realized a good many years afterwards how lucky I had been that I didn't have the censorship at the back of my mind because two things then would happen to you. One was that you would write in order to get past the censors; therefore, you would suppress certain truths which you think should have been told. The other one was that you would do something in order to shock them, and both these attitudes would upset the artistic balance. I wrote my first book in perfect ignorance of the Censorship Board. It never occurred to me.

Looking back, how do you think you wiped the Censorship Board out of your mind?

I never lived in that atmosphere. While I wouldn't say my family were liberal by any means, they didn't read all that much, so they weren't interested in the Censorship Board.

What sort of response did you get from your family when *The Pilgrimage* was banned?

They didn't respond at all. They said nothing. Nobody belonging to me—my mother, my uncles, my cousins, anyone belonging to me —they never mentioned any of my books to me, ever. Not ever. I think it was because they disapproved. Quite apart from everything else, they would disapprove of a writer in the family, even if he just wrote children's books; they would think it was a waste of time. Only fallen women went on the stage: that was an idea at one time, very Victorian, in Ireland. Waste of time. Make much more money baking buns.

What about the Athlone community? How did it respond?

Nobody ever said anything to me about it. There was one lady who did say something to my mother about it. My mother came back considerably distressed, and she said this lady, who is dead now, had said something to her about my book. I said, "What did she say?" "Oh, she asked me did I read it, and I said, 'No.' She said, 'Well, of course, it's a dreadful book, and I'm terribly surprised at John writing a book like that.'" I went down to this woman, and I read the riot act to her. I said, "I don't mind you saying anything to me personally because I'm quite able to take care of myself. I will not have you interfering with my family or anyone belonging to me. And you know," I said, "as far as banned books are concerned, if you thought you could get a man, you would walk naked down Church Street."

Were you ever discriminated against in Athlone?

I know that some idiot put me up for the County Club in Athlone, and they wouldn't have me although my uncles were members and my grandfather was a member. "No, we won't have his sort in here." I wouldn't have joined them. I've never joined a club in my life except the Automobile Club in Dublin. That was to park the car. I'm not a clubbable man.

Were you ever harassed in any other way after _The Pilgrimage_ was banned?

I think I was privately in certain libraries. I think there was a certain group of people who had a considerable influence on the libraries and perhaps on the bookshops who tried through the Censorship Board to prevent people reading *The Pilgrimage,* in particular, and subsequently by private censorship afterwards. I think there are a few places in which even now there would be certain prejudice against me in libraries. The Longford-Westmeath Library were very enlightened about me. I knew the librarians in there, and they certainly did their best to keep *The Pilgrimage* in circulation for those who wanted it until it was unbanned. It very much depends upon the local parish priest, you know.

I remember when Father Peter Connolly, who died last year, was lecturer in English at Maynooth. He was an old friend of mine. He invited me in to speak to his class, and the president of Maynooth said, "Oh, no, no. We can't have him; he's a writer of salacious books. We can't have him in here." Then about six months afterwards his appointment as parish priest, or whatever it was, was announced, and there was a new president, and he didn't seem to mind my books. He was all very friendly with me anyway. Peter rang me up to say, "Well, we want you to come in to dinner on the old president's last night." No, he didn't say that. It was afterwards I heard it, or I wouldn't have gone. "We want you to come in to dinner on Saturday night." I went in, and there was a reception room, and the old president was there with his red sash. I shook hands with him, and he was quite civil and so on. It was only afterwards I heard that it was a conspiracy of the liberal wing to get me in before he left.

Peter Connolly was a very important voice against censorship.[2]

Yes, he was. He was a wonderful man.

Your family had a very secure social and economic position in Athlone. Do you think that protected you in any way?

I've said this several times before; this is not new. If I were a schoolteacher or librarian in Athlone at that time, I couldn't possibly have written that book and published it. I would have met the same fate as John McGahern. But, you see, we were pretty large employers in the town and large ratepayers. I came from a very highly respectable family because they had money. That was the way to achieve respect in Ireland: was to have money. Nothing could be done to me because, I suppose, of the staff and the general setup in the town.

It gave you a great deal of freedom as a writer, didn't it?

Yes, I suppose it did, yes. Well, it gave me the freedom to travel for one thing and to live outside that mentality. I didn't have that mentality.

Didn't it also give you the freedom to write?

Yes, it did.

Do you think that writers who didn't have your economic security were more vulnerable?

There was one writer, in particular, a woman called Norah Hoult.

A number of her books were banned by the Censorship Board.

She was a very good short story writer, and she died in Delgany with nothing except the old-age pension. I had some correspondence with her before she died, and she was very shaky and that kind of thing. I made inquiries, and they told me she was living in a small cottage in Delgany, and she was very, very poor, but very religious. She was a convert to Catholicism, and so she didn't make any complaints. Indeed, she had a lot to complain about. She was a most distinguished writer. She ended up in great poverty, and nobody bothered their head about it.

Are you aware of any writers whose work was seriously affected by the presence of the Censorship Board?

There was a very good Irish novelist called Francis MacManus who wrote a wonderful book, *The Fire in the Dust.* It was about Kilkenny. Wonderful book. Now, he was afraid of the Censorship Board, and he deliberately wrote and suppressed certain things in his books. He was head of features in Radio Eireann.

Do you think MacManus was afraid of losing his job?

I think he was afraid. He had a rather sad private life. His first wife died, and he was left with a son who had an insufficient heart and was therefore a cripple. Frank was very devoted to him, as people are to children like that. He married again, and then he died suddenly, just like that, when he was fifty-six. Strain, I'd say. Then his second wife told me—I was asking her about the boy. She said, "Oh, I'm having a terrible time with him. The doctor advised me to send him to the university because he was very clever, because keeping him at home like that was not going to help. He will die young anyway." He made two suicide attempts afterwards. He threw himself downstairs, and he tried to kill himself with the kitchen knife. She was in a state. You can imagine the state she was in. She came home from work one evening and found him dead in the same chair in which his father died. Very sad. I think the Censorship Board is very largely responsible for that because of the strain the man was under. He couldn't write freely because he had to have a job. He couldn't afford to get his name in the paper as "indecent or obscene" with a son like that he had to support.

Do you think many people were affected like that?

I'm sure they were. I'm sure their home lives were affected because people have to be protective towards children. Very often a man will write something which his wife mightn't approve of or the other way around.

You say that censorship made writers fearful. Do you think that it also made them more critical of Irish society?

Yes, I think it would have that effect because if you saw books which you could afford to buy in London—because in those days the customs officials, unless it was *Lady Chatterley's Lover* or something like that which had been publicized, wouldn't know—you could bring back books that were banned. If you read these books and realized how very inoffensive they were, then you'd ask yourself what sort of people ban books like this.

And what conclusion would you come to?

I think the first thing that would strike you was that there was a great deal of hypocrisy in it and a great deal of ignorance about fundamental human rights and a great deal of arrogance about fundamental human rights and a great deal of self-righteousness. And, of course, it was very, very stupid ultimately. Self-righteousness and arrogance and all these associated emotions: they're nearly all negative ones.

I'd like to return to the subject of attitudes toward sexuality. You spoke earlier about sexual narrow-mindedness, saying that sex was a taboo subject when you were growing up. Just how taboo was it?

It's quite extraordinary the lengths people would go to avoid talking about anything of that kind. For instance, if somebody mentioned Oscar Wilde in company, people would say, "Well, who was he?" Or they would say, "Oh, wasn't he that man who was mixed up with some awful case in England?" If you had the temerity to say, "Well, what was the case? What did he do?" They would say, "Well, we don't really know. It was something awful." They wouldn't even mention it.

There must have been a great deal of sexual ignorance.

Oh, yes. Yes, yes. It was very, very hard on women.

It was unusual for an Irish writer to write about homosexuality in the early sixties. What kind of response did you get to the homosexual content of *The Pilgrimage*?

Well, it was banned. One pretty well known critic said that a more unpleasant collection of characters had never been gathered within the boards of an Irish novel—that kind of thing. Of course, there's always a double standard in Ireland, and people went to Belfast and bought it. They went to London and bought it. Everyone who wanted to read it, read it.

Even today a significant number of the books that are banned deal with the subject of homosexuality. In general, what do you think is the Irish attitude toward homosexuality?

I think the Irish are pathological about homosexuality. That was one of the reasons why I chose it as the theme for my books because it never had been done before. It existed in a small way in the bourgeoisie in Ireland. I think probably much more now. But it was one of the things which was absolutely unspeakable and which they would never admit to, so if you wanted to hit them, that was where to hit them.

How do you account for the fact that your other novels weren't banned?

It's because of the whole sexual interest in my books. They don't want that to be made public. I think they came to the conclusion that this unmentionable subject was dealt with, and the less publicity that they got the better. They were becoming a little more intelligent than they had been. I think that was the reason. I don't think that my books will be generally discussed in Ireland until I'm dead. They're almost pathological about it, but it's different when the author's dead. If Proust had lived into 1930, his book certainly would not have been allowed in Ireland. I don't know whether it was banned or not; it might be one of the ones that they had never heard of. Anyway, it's so long. He's now discussed quite openly in universities. And Wilde is, but it would not have happened in Wilde's lifetime. I think that they're very inhibited while I'm still alive. It's a continued censorship.

You also have written about the sexual lives of priests. What kind of response did you get to that subject matter?

None of the priests are homosexual, by the way, in any of my books because I didn't know any homosexual priests. There are, but I don't happen to know any. *An Apology for Roses,* which was the first novel to deal with a priest having an affair since George Moore's *The Lake,* was a best seller in Ireland. It sold and sold and sold for about three years. I think it's still in demand in the libraries. That's how they reacted to that. Everyone thought it would be banned, but again it wasn't.

You said earlier that you wrote without ever thinking about the Censorship Board. Did you ever have any communication with the board?

No, not with the board. I didn't even know who was on it.

Did you ever appeal *The Pilgrimage*?

No, no.

Why not?

Well, I don't think you can appeal to people that are as stupid and narrow-minded as that. You would recognize them by appealing, wouldn't you?

You'd recognize their authority and their right to ban books.

I didn't think they had that moral right, so it would never occur to me to appeal. I wouldn't have anything to do with people of that sort.

The Irish Writer in Exile

To what degree do you think Ireland alienated its writers by banning their books?

I think it alienated them more by its disapproval and its contempt and its lack of enthusiasm. Joyce hated Ireland for that because they were so narrow-minded and because of the way his books were suppressed in Ireland. You know, the Jesuits kept them locked up in drawers where he was educated. Once his wife Nora wanted to come back to Galway—she was a Barnacle from Galway—and he said, "You want to be very, very careful. They'll throw vitriol in your face in Ireland if they know who you are."

It was a very closed society, and after the Free State came into being, there weren't any of the literary at homes there used to be in the old days with Lady Fingall and Maud Gonne, and there were several more like that. It was Padraic Colum told me about that. They lingered on into the twenties, but they were nearly all finished by the thirties. The new Catholic zealots had taken over, and there was no real literary social life in Ireland. Ireland was a much freer place when the British were there. The society was more open. The zealots, the narrow-minded Opus Dei, Legion of Mary people took over.

You've lived outside Ireland for quite some time.

Of recent years wholly outside.

Did a desire to escape a censorship mentality have anything to do with your leaving?

Ireland is a very incestuous country in the sense that it's a small population. We all know one another. If you meet someone in a train travelling from Galway to Dublin and you get talking to them, it's almost certain that somewhere along the line they're going to know somebody you know. You have this sense of being watched all the time as a result in Ireland. It's a psychological sense. In small towns like Athlone it's very acute. I gave a description of this woman walking through the town—which is based on Athlone, though it's not—and the sense she had of being watched. This is death to writers because it interferes with your psychological and intellectual freedom. It interferes even with your physical freedom in a way.

So you feel a lack of privacy in Ireland.

There's an invasion of privacy in Ireland, a psychological invasion of privacy which you don't have here.

Does that affect your writing?

Yes, it does.

In what kind of way?

It's freer and kindlier and funnier. I can look back, not in anger, but with a laugh. I think you've got to experience it at the beginning; you've got to live among all that kind of thing. It was a bit like the Puritans in America, wasn't it? You know, *The Crucible* by Arthur Miller and *The Scarlet Letter.* It was exactly the same sort of society as that. It did produce some very good literature. You have to live with that to experience exactly what kind it is, but there comes a time when you have to get out.

In your novels you describe Ireland as being a very self-destructive country. Do you think it's particularly so for its writers?

Yes, yes. It's a good country to die in. You can always get a good funeral in Ireland, but it's not a good country to live in. It's a country of enormous funerals. Priests, policemen, publicans, and politicians.

Ireland Today

Do you think censorship still poses a threat in Ireland today?

Well, I am a little bit alarmed that it's still active and particularly about *The Erotic Art of India.* If you can afford to go to India, you can see these things in temples. You can see them in Pompeii if you can afford to go to Naples. And there are lots of other places where there are erotic drawings and carvings. I think it's disgraceful that it should still be active. It's silly and stupid and prehistoric.

Are you surprised that it's still active?

I'm surprised, yes, considering what's going on in Ireland in daylight.

Why do you think censorship has retained its hold in Ireland for such a long time?

I think it's part of the government process. They feel that, as a Catholic country, they should make some stand against the rising tide of pornography. But there is always an excuse for a Censorship Board. We must protect our young; the young are being raped on the streets. We must protect our old; the old are being murdered in their beds, are frightened out of their wits by bullyboys with knives. What's the good of censorship? Of course, you know, there's a big drift to the right in every country.

There is in Ireland, particularly in the area of sexual morality. Groups such as the Society for the Protection of the Unborn Child have become quite powerful.

They're like the Opus Dei. Well, I don't believe in any secret societies like that, from the Freemasons to the Knights of Columbanus. I don't believe in any secret societies like that. I think that they are always wrong and that they always serve one section of the community against the benefit of others.

Do you see them as reflecting a kind of censorship mentality?

I think they do, yes.

Would you say, then, that there is an official censorship exercised by the Censorship Board and an unofficial censorship that is equally as strong?

I think it's more insidious because at least the censorship is there and it's an official body, and nowadays with human rights in Strasbourg and The Hague, you can take an action against things like that. In the old days people were helpless, but now we've come on a little more, and people are better supported by international organizations.[3] The unofficial censorship—no one can do anything about it because it's hidden.

Would you say that's very characteristic of Ireland?

Yes, I think it is characteristic. Secret societies are very characteristic of Ireland: they always were. Also, they just don't like literary people. They think they're foolish and wicked and immoral and that they don't make enough money. It hasn't security like the civil service. You must go into the civil service because at the end of it you'll get a pension.

What do you think is the future for censorship in Ireland?

They didn't succeed. They didn't succeed with anyone. They won't succeed with Alex Comfort. They won't succeed with anyone like that. It's hopeless. Anyway, Ireland's geographical situation is such that with the border there, you can bring bombs and you can bring books, equally dangerous to the Southern mind.

The Principle of Censorship

What is your attitude toward censorship as a matter of principle?

I don't believe in censorship at all. If you draw the line, you run into trouble immediately. Where do you draw the line? I think censorship should be something for an adult.

JOHN MCGAHERN

John McGahern was born in Dublin in 1935 and reared in County Roscommon. His second novel, *The Dark,* was banned in 1965 by the Irish Censorship Board. The novel created a sensation when it appeared because the word "fuck" is used on the first page, and there are descriptions of a boy masturbating. McGahern was fired from his job as a primary school teacher after the novel was banned, and his case became so controversial that it was raised in the Irish Parliament. His other fiction includes *The Leave-taking* (1974), *The Pornographer* (1979), and *High Ground* (1986). McGahern lives in County Leitrim, where he was interviewed by Julia Carlson for Article 19 on 27 September 1987.

The Personal Experience
of Censorship

I'd like to talk first about what happened when *The Dark* was banned. It probably was the most controversial of all the bannings, wasn't it?

I suppose it was. They banned it first, and then I got sacked as a teacher. It was in the papers every day, so there was enormous controversy about it. There weren't many literary prizes then, and I was the possessor of the only two state prizes—the AE Award and the Macauley—for *The Barracks*. In a way I was almost an official writer when *The Dark* was banned.

What was your personal reaction when the book was banned?

I didn't really care for myself because it was something of the time. If you were a writer, you half expected it; there actually would be no shock or surprise. It was something that you lived with. You wrote the way you wanted to anyhow.

Would you have been pleased?

No. I remember being friendly with the English writer Joe Ackerley at the time, and he said to me, "That's great news; you'll get a lot of publicity, and it'll increase sales." Odd enough, that's not the way I felt because, in that sense, one has a family in Ireland, and it was quite a social disgrace.

You mean literally a family?

Yes, my brothers and sisters.

How did they respond to it?

I think that they were upset and that they were struggling. Then my father, when I didn't seem to be defending myself—he was naturally belligerent anyhow—was springing to my defense, which would be a greater disaster than any enemy.

When *The Barracks* was published, my aunt had a sweetshop beside the school in Ballinamore, and the priest in charge of the school removed my book from the public library in the town on his own authority. The reason was that a married couple had made love in affectionate tiredness on Christmas evening, and he took this as unfit for consumption. She told him that if he took John's books out of the library, he could buy his cigarettes elsewhere. In that sense, the local or the personal would always be stronger.

Tell me about the loss of your job. First of all, how did you find out that you had lost your job?

I had a leave of absence without pay, and I was made several approaches on the grapevine not to come back to the school, that I would be doing everybody a favour. It was called doing the decent: "Don't attempt to take up your job." Since I was a good teacher, I got every encouragement that they'd write glowing references for a job in England, but not to come back there to disturb. That made me twice as determined.

Who made these approaches to you on the grapevine?

The headmaster, mostly, who was really working on behalf of the clerical authorities and the parish priest.[1] It turned out that he was taking direct orders from the archbishop of Dublin, John Charles McQuaid. The archbishop was behind the whole thing, and he had an absolute obsession about what he called impure books.

I saw that the only way to effect anything was to turn up physically and report to the headmaster. On the day I was supposed to go back, I just got the bus out as normal and turned up at the school. I had been teaching with these people for seven or eight years; it was a relatively small school. Everybody was in a state of absolute dismay—including myself. Everybody was absolutely frightened. We must have drank gallons of tea in the teachers' room. They were all in to see me. The headmaster was in a shocking state and asked me why did I come. I said, "Well, I have to get some explanation." He tried to say that I was no longer employed, and I said, "I am employed." I actually showed him the terms of my contract. Then—they obviously had foreseen that—he took out a letter saying that I was suspended from entering the classroom. Typically, the parish priest had gone on his holidays, so there was no way to contact him.

I had to go back to England, and then when the parish priest returned from his holidays, I had to come back and get an interview with him. He asked me what did I want to write books for and why did I want to bring trouble, that their phone had been annoyed with journalists and that he also heard that I was married and didn't get married in a church. It took me a long time to get any letter of why I was dismissed, and the only letter I got said: "Mr. McGahern is well aware of the reason of his dismissal." It was priceless!

Did he actually say that the banning of *The Dark* was behind the loss of your job?

Yes, he did. He actually said it was the archbishop. He was quite clear.

What kind of response did you get from your fellow teachers?

The BBC did a programme on me and the business at the time, and I got up to eight or nine letters from teachers that had been fired for fairly trivial offenses while really running foul of the parish priest. These were in Birmingham, I remember, and Glasgow and were teaching there. They had no recourse at all; they just had to leave, and there was no publicity or anything.

What about the teachers you worked with? Were they supportive of you in your case?

No, they'd be frightened. What made it twice as ironical was that a year before, our school—the school I was teaching in—got the Carlisle and Blake Premium. It's an award for teaching. Generally it was a three- or four-teacher school got it. It was very unusual for a school that big—there were fourteen teachers—because it required that every teacher had to be not only efficient but highly efficient. It was a very, very good school, and it was a very hard-working school. It was a big shock for everybody.

Do you think you were more vulnerable as a teacher than you would have been in some other occupation?

Oh, definitely. Definitely. It was brought up in the Dail, and the leader of the Labour party, Corish, I think, at the time, said it was an incredible system: that while the state paid for the teachers, it was the church hired and fired them. I remember when I was a young teacher in 1955, and I used to go away for weekends, which you were entitled to. I used to go to Dublin to escape the small provincial town I was teaching in. I was told I could lose my job if I wouldn't stay at home—which I ignored at the time—for teaching catechism after Mass on a Sunday, which wasn't part of my duties at all. It was a very strange time.

The point is—I committed no statutory offense. The book was banned, but that's not an offense. I was not molesting children. It was said by the Irish National Teachers' Organisation at the time that I needed to believe in order to inculcate a faith, and I argued that I didn't need to believe. All I needed was knowledge and skill. You know, and you could teach that a donkey had round legs.

Did you get any response from the parents of your students?

There is this contradiction in Ireland—that the personal will almost always prevail over the ideological. In fact, the only people that kicked up ructions were the parents of the children I was teaching. They were very annoyed because, simply, I was a good teacher, and the children were fond of me. They were the only people that caused a lot of trouble in my support. It was very flattering at the time. It really didn't matter about anybody else in a way.

You took your case to the Irish National Teachers' Organisation, didn't you? What happened when you did?

Once I actually decided to face into it, it was embarrassing and painful. My instinct was to go away, which I was asked to do, and not to disturb things and be a nice fellow. Really, I just felt I was being manipulated, and once I did face in, I was going to see it through to the end.

The Irish National Teachers' Organisation got out of it on a technicality. I had been abroad for a year. People often lapsed their dues for two or three years because the membership, the union dues, are collected in the school every quarter generally by the equivalent of a shop steward. I couldn't have paid because I was out of the country, and I wasn't teaching. As soon as I reported at school, that activated my union membership, but they said that my union membership had lapsed because I was a year in arrears, which was suspending me from membership on a technicality. That's the reason they gave—that I was no longer a member—but I met the whole executive.

There was a man who is dead since at the meeting, and he was quite drunk in the early afternoon. He said this funny thing that I have quoted since. He said, "If it was just the banned book, then we might have been able to do something for you, though it would have been difficult. But with marrying this woman, you're an impossible case." He says, "By the way, McGahern, what entered your head to go and marry a foreign woman when there's hundreds of thousands of Irish women going around with their tongues out for a husband!" I'll never forget that phrase—"with their tongues out for a husband." I was busily chasing girls, but I never saw anything as delicious as that going around. I just asked academic questions. "If I regularized my relationship"—all I had to do was get married in the Catholic church—"would that be all right?" He says, "On no account. Don't you know that many's the priest down the country who would sack you for even marrying a Protestant in a Catholic church?" So there was absolutely nothing I could do.

Then I heard privately, but there was no way you could prove this, that John Charles McQuaid said if the Irish National Teachers' Organisation backed me, he wouldn't give them any support in pay negotiations that were coming up for the department, and that he'd back them to the hilt if they would have nothing to do with my case. Naturally, a whole pay negotiation is much more important than a single teacher. But some of the Irish National Teachers' Organisation members were quite indignant, and some of them suspended their membership. I just knew a few of them who weren't literary people but felt that I had been blackguarded.

You mentioned earlier that your case was brought up in the Dail. It was Owen Sheehy Skeffington who took up your case, wasn't it? How did you feel when it became a popular cause?

I admired Sheehy Skeffington, and you couldn't get a more decent person. He really was just interested in the rights or wrongs. He wasn't interested in making capital of it. He wrote an article in *Censorship,* and he said he got a lot of abusive letters.[2]

Do you think that other people who took up your case were interested in making capital of it?

Yes, I do. It's not very pleasant to reflect because one doesn't know, but I think that they were much more interested in attracting light to themselves than in the moral issues. That was a sort of fashionable thing, like a suit of clothes. There was a whole lot of people jumping on the bandwagon, too, serious people. For instance, I got sent a ticket to turn up with Edna O'Brien at the Gate Theatre for an anticensorship meeting, and I refused to go to that because I felt I was being used.

I did say at the time that I had no expectation that I would get my job, but that I wanted the facts of the case out in the open, and people could make up their own minds about the justice or injustice of it. Then I was approached privately by somebody on behalf of the Civil Liberties to see would I be interested in taking the case to the High Court, but the way I saw it, all I had to do was put the case clearly, and I had managed to do that. I also got advice from a lawyer who said that it would be very unlikely I'd win the case, given the climate of opinion at that time in the High Court.

There's a sort of interesting story. Professor O Briain from Galway was on the Appeal Board at the time. He was professor of French, and he was a friend of Con Leventhal in Paris. Leventhal had been a reader of French in Trinity, and he retired to go and stay

with Beckett in Paris. He and Beckett wanted to write protesting.
Beckett read the book first and said he'd be glad to support it, but
he says, "You must ask McGahern if he wants a petition." I actually
said I didn't for the reason that I thought that the case was put
clearly enough and that people could make up their own minds. He
was the only person that really thought of asking me if I wanted to
have a petition, and I said, no. When O Briain came to Paris and
they were having dinner, Leventhal said to him, "What in the name
of God is wrong with you in Ireland banning McGahern's books?
Will nothing else do?" O Briain was very defensive at this stage,
and he says, "Well, we can't have people running round the country
with their flies open!"

**You lived in London for quite a number of years after *The
Dark* was banned. Could you have gotten work in Ireland
after the banning of the book?**

No, I couldn't get a job, unless I got into RTE or something like
that. It would be very, very difficult for me to have lived in Dublin
at that time because the couple of times I went back I was recognized everywhere. People were arguing my case on "The Late Late
Show." I was in the newspapers every day. My photograph was all
over the place. I stayed in London for several years after that; I just
had to make a living. One was very lucky that one actually could go
to England and that one's books sold in England.

**What kind of effect did the banning of *The Dark* have on your
writing?**

I didn't manage to write for three or four years after the business.

Why not?

You never know. You may not have been able to write anything anyhow. The unpleasant thing about both the banning and the sacking
was that—for the writer all that matters is whether the work is
good or bad—it brought something prurient into it, which for me
has nothing to do with whether a work is good or bad. It confused

the issue, and one also found that one was a sort of public figure from just being a writer, and there's some people that enjoy that, and I don't.

Do you think censorship prompted Irish writers to look at Irish society more critically?

I don't think so. I wrote always because I needed to write. I needed to—that's the way I wanted to think and see for myself, and, of course, it was the enormous generality and comfort that reading gave one. I mean that one was going to attempt the thing oneself sooner or later. But one was just going to see. One never thought one would be published. I think that when a writer is writing, he's actually interested in getting his sentences right, and he really never thinks of the effect. The only time I was on "The Gay Byrne Show," he actually asked me did I not think about putting in certain spicy bits that would make me famous. I said, "If you ever wrote sentences and paragraphs, you would have enough to do to keep the rhythm and images and grammar in order without thinking about whether it would make you famous or not." I think most writers actually think that they live in a totally free world while they're working. The whole thing of censorship is like the marketing and publication of a book, which I see as a completely different activity than the act of writing.

Do you think that censorship ever served as a spur to creativity for Irish writers?

No. I wouldn't think it hindered it either. I think a writer will unconsciously reflect his society. If you want to have a cleaner literature, first of all you have to get a cleaner society. Cleaning up literature is actually putting the cart before the horse.

The Irish Literary Community

What kind of impact do you think that censorship had upon the literary community in Ireland?

I think there's still very little sense of a literary community in Ireland.

Why?

The amazing thing is that it's a Catholic country and that nearly all the writers are not Catholics. They're lapsed Catholics. I think that the church in Ireland was peculiarly antiintellectual, say, compared to the French church. People like Mauriac or Bloy could have no place here. It was a very simple world of the GAA [Gaelic Athletic Association] and the drama society with a very distorted view of life.[3]

Do you think that censorship was part of this antiintellectualism?

Yes, except I think that it's part of the whole sexuality. It was a young, insecure state without any traditions, without any manners, and there was this notion that to be Irish was good. Nobody actually took any time to understand what to be Irish was. There was this slogan and fanaticism and a lot of emotion, but there wasn't any clear idea except what you were against: you were against sexuality; you were against the English. There was this tendency which I actually resented in Dublin literary society when I grew up—I mean the first time I would have entered it—that one was much more defined by what one was against than by what one was for. So it was safe to attack a book as rubbish but quite dangerous to say you actually liked a book and admired it. You often found that people were attacking people like Lawrence, and they hadn't read him at all. "Lawrence? Rubbish."

One of the things that I resent about my upbringing is that the doctrine was taught to us by celibates, and the very nature of abstinence is that it makes food or whatever it is more attractive than if you have too much of it. I actually think that it elevated a normal human appetite into an importance that distorted the reality of almost the whole of life. I think it was a very dangerous thing and a very twisted thing: the whole attitude to sexuality. I see censorship as just a symptom of something that was much more dangerous and inhuman and, I would say, certainly fascistic in the real sense of the word.

What do you think the Irish attitude is toward the writer?

I think the writer is feared here because I think, in a way, that he's one of the only uncompromised moral authorities. It's such a small community that the politicians and the journalists and the church, to a certain extent, are compromised. I think while the church influences society, in a way, a society gets whatever church and politicians it deserves. There was cultivation of sexlessness here as well because of the bachelor, simply because it wasn't economically possible for him to marry until the parents grew too old. Celibacy was admired because of economic necessity, and, of course, the church came and copperfastened that.

What do you think of Ireland as a place for the writer to live?

The whole thing that I really resented when I was young was that you had to go into exile if you were an Irish writer, like Joyce and Beckett. In a way, I was the first generation of people who were born into an independent state, and I always had the feeling I was a citizen of this state, that there was no need to be anti-English. I had no intellectual inferiority when I met English writers. I think that it's our country, and one should make the best of it. I think there's a lot to be desired about it. It's a much more healthy society than I grew up in. There are people prepared to stand up and be counted, and people are less afraid.

Ireland Today

Do you find that you're still looked upon as a banned writer today?

Somebody was looking for me and asked my neighbour, "Do you know where John McGahern lives?" She says, "Isn't that the fella

that writes the dirty books?" He said, "Did you read them?" "Oh,"
she says, "no, I wouldn't read them." He said, "How do you know
that they're dirty?" And she said, "Oh, everybody says that they're
dirty."

I was in Enniskillen during the right-to-life debates here [in
1983].[4] This doctor I used to know when I was in Dublin came up to
me, and I suppose I hadn't seen the man in twenty years. He sailed
up to me, and he says, "I suppose you're for abortion." I said to
myself, this is a nice how-do-you-do after twenty years. I says, "As
a matter of fact, I am." So he says, "You believe in killing babies."
I says, "Nothing of the kind." This sort of argument went on. I just
meant that if anybody wanted to have an abortion, that they should
be able to get an abortion. It's a load of hypocrisy because you are
only discriminating against the ignorant or the very poor, because
anybody with a few pounds in their pocket can go to England and
have an abortion. I said, "The whole matter is academic." He let an
enormous roar at me. He says, "It's the principle of the thing that
matters."

**What about the right-wing pressure groups that have risen
up now? Do you see a similarity between the kind of mentality that gave rise to the censorship and the mentality that
has given rise to these groups?**

Yes. I think it's more difficult for them now, but I think that in
the beginning it was a very young and insecure state, and there
was a whole vacuum in the leadership of society. It was filled by
the church—I think that's sociologically true—and by the medical
society. Doctors and priests actually became the new aristocrats
and leaders of fashion. There was this whole mentality—with the
economic war in England—that if we could build this fascist, blue-
blood Irish race and that if everybody learned Irish and knew no
English, that all foreign corrupting influences would be kept out. I
think censorship was a kind of by-product of that mentality, and I
would see the abortion debate as the same thing, as basically fascist and insular, an attempt to isolate society so it will conform to
a very limited, narrow idea of itself.

You say you think the right-wing groups have more trouble now. Would you say the society is less monolithic?

Yes, I think education is less elitist now. More people get educated. In my time unless you were in the middle class or you got scholarships—and there were only two for every county—you never had a chance of getting to university. Very, very few people got even to secondary school, so people were much more ignorant. There was a powerful unofficial censorship when I was growing up. The new middle class, which was mostly the priest and the doctor, was antiintellectual. There was something considered wrong and dangerous and idle about reading books. The only purpose for reading books was to pass exams, which would get you a job, which would get you on in the world. For instance, when I was in training college, and that's not all that long ago, 1953 to 1955, four or five boys founded a little debating society, and they were nicknamed Oideachas Eireann, which is awfully sarcastic: it translates "The Higher Institute of Irish Learning." They were absolutely hounded in the place. These were people nineteen and twenty, and they were going to go out and teach and would be leaders of most rural communities. This fellow would prowl up and down the study hall, and if you were reading Eliot or some book that wasn't on the course, you could actually get biffed at the back of your ears.

In the sense of the mentality at the time, there was a very funny case of a bookseller in Galway. The bookseller had a special request for a special customer—we often wondered was it the bishop of Galway—and Fabers were to send him a copy of *The Dark* with these instructions: number one, tear off the dust jacket and throw it in the wastepaperbasket; tear the spine off the book and throw that into the wastepaperbasket; tear the book in two; place both halves of the book in separate plain brown envelopes; number five was, I think, will pay whether they arrive or not. That's for a very special customer. That was what the bookseller's letter had, and Fabers actually photostated a copy and sent it to me, which I have still. So you can get the mentality at the time.

Do you think censorship is still a threat today?

I don't think so at all. Anybody that wants to buy books can get them anyhow, and I think it's just seen as comic bungling. We're lucky enough in the sense that we belong to the English-speaking world, which is a large culture, and no matter how they try, they can't isolate a small place like this.

I think in a way it was a peculiarly isolated movement, the puritanical movement, still is now. It's actually a couple of narrow ideologues, and they really haven't much contact with the roots of the country who couldn't care less, who know how they have to sell a few cows or emigrate.

The Principle of Censorship

What is your attitude toward censorship as a matter of principle?

I actually think that censorship is a self-defeating thing. Nearly all forbidden things are attractive by definition, so it is the most nonsensical law because it has its own in-built self-destruction in it. If you ban a thing, you actually draw more attention to it, so you wind up by doing the opposite. A book should be judged on whether it's entertaining or whether it's useful or whether it's well written. I actually happen to think that if something is well written, it can't but be moral by definition. It's self-defeating; I mean it's actually stupid.

Do you see any time when censorship should be exercised?

I was asked that in California, in Berkeley, by the IRA over the section.[5] I would actually say, no, but on the other hand, if there is an organization without authority that's dedicated to the overthrow of the state and goes round murdering people, then if the state decides not to give them publicity, one has to admit that the state has a point.

E D N A   O' B R I E N

Edna O'Brien was born in Tuamgraney, County Clare.
Virtually all of her fiction published during the 1960s
was banned by the Irish Censorship Board, including *The
Country Girls* (1960), *The Lonely Girl* (1962), *Girl with the
Green Eyes* (1964), *Girls in Their Married Bliss* (1964),
August Is a Wicked Month (1965), and *Casualties of Peace*
(1966), and she was strongly attacked for having betrayed
Irish womanhood. O'Brien was one of the few writers of
her generation to protest against censorship in Ireland.
She spoke at public meetings and publicly brought her
books into the country across the border from Northern
Ireland. Her most recent novel is *The High Road* (1988).
Since 1959 O'Brien has lived in London, where she was
interviewed by Julia Carlson for Article 19 on 11 May 1988.

The Personal Experience of Censorship

The vehemence of the language that was used to criticize your work suggests that it touched a deep nerve in Ireland in the 1960s.[1] Do you think that's true?

Yes, I think it did. I wasn't aware of it, thank God, while I was writing the books because it would have paralyzed me. I think it did strike a chord for several reasons. One was I was a woman and, indeed, a girl. I was in my twenties, and I think they were shocked that a girl would have written a novel at all. The other thing is I love literature, real literature, but I hate what I call literary stuff, and my book was not literary in that sense. The language is very natural. I like natural prose, so they were able to understand it. What I wanted to say, I said, as truly as I could say it at that time. So there was no gloss. I think it was that I tried to eschew hypocrisy and stage-Irish rigamarole. I'm bored with rigamarole. I don't want rigamarole. I don't want to write it, and I don't want to read it.

Do you think people were disturbed by your treatment of women?

I think so, yes. I think so because it was about the covert and the not-so-covert, rather foolish sexuality of two young girls. It was their romance and their sexuality because Baba was sex and Cait was romance. I admitted their sexuality, also unhappy married life —a young girl yearning and, indeed, eventually having sex with a much older married man. *Girls in Their Married Bliss* horrified them completely. Indeed, it was very funny. When it was published, I was really savaged. They all said that I had lost my lyrical quality. In fact, now, twenty-five years later, *Girls in Their Married Bliss* stands up. It has some guts. But I did have a very rough time on two levels. On the public level, being banned, and on a more personal level.

Were you hurt in other ways when your books were banned —by your family or by the community in which you were reared?

Very much. You know, a bit of affirmation either from the family or the community helps a lot, especially when you start off. I had none. My own family, my mother and father, God rest them, were appalled. Everyone in the village was. I got anonymous letters about sewers and sewerage and all that innuendo!

Was your family very hostile?

They were ashamed, so I was ashamed and believed I had done something awful.

Why did you feel a sense of shame?

One gets very confused, you know, by accusations. I was young, and I was frightened, still am to a great extent! If people tell you you've written dirt, even if you know you haven't, some of it stays with you. I wanted to go away very far. Australia even.

You mentioned that everyone in your village was appalled. Exactly how did people respond to the banning of your books?

I'm sure if I'd lived in Dublin, let's say, or come from Dublin, the reaction might have been a little more mixed because Dublin's full of contrary people for a start, and they would just take sides. In my own village one person would tell me what another person had said. They'd pass on the bad news about how dirty it was. There's one little joke, however. The first book was banned, and all were duly horrified. The second book came, and they had apoplexy. One woman said to me, "You know," she said, "we're beginning to think that the first book was a prayer book by comparison." Some woman who had read it got terribly ill and felt she was possessed by the devil, and the priest had to come to her house. There were a few copies of it burned in the chapel grounds. It all belongs to the Middle Ages, don't you think?

It bruised me, of course. But I'm not bitter; bitterness is boring. You know, the things that happen to you like that wound you, but you kind of put them away in a secret drawer of your mind.

I think censorship was always much more severe in rural Ireland.

Understandably. People know each other's lives. But to write it is taboo. Then if you write in a kind of personal tone, as I do, they assume without any shadow of doubt that everything in it happened to you. They don't understand that the soul of a book like *A Portrait of the Artist as a Young Man* or even, to a lesser extent, *The Country Girls* springs from a fusion of fact, feeling and imagination. People are constantly asking, Is it autobiographical? I said, "Well, I'd be a goner now if I did everything I wrote."

Do you think it made a difference that you were so attractive?

Probably. I mean, I'm not that attractive, but on a good day I can muster it.

You were in a sense physically the image—

—of the colleen. Yes, yes. More codology, that sort of colleen image, being very pretty and unblemished, sitting at the hearth. Funnily enough, the so-called image makes a difference in England, too. I don't choose my own photographs for my cover; the publishers get a nice photograph because they want to; but again and again some snide remarks crop up. That infuriates me. If you happen to have your hair done, well, then you can't be a serious writer. It's so narrow, really.

Why do you think you spark off such resentment?

Oh, appearing to be attractive and giving the notion of maybe having a wonderful life. I wish I had! Grudge prevails all over the world; it isn't just in Ireland.

But envy is very strong in Ireland, especially in the small, enclosed rural communities.

In Dublin's fair city, too. God, they get the razors out. Some hostility is also to do with my being a bit of a hermit: not playing the social game. I don't go to parties. I live a secluded life. People really resent that. Writing is my life, my existence, not only how I earn my living, but also my inner existence. It's my everything—that and my children.

Do you think that the banning of your books had any artistic effect on your work?

A bit. Writing is in itself such a frightening thing that that kind of semipunishment (it isn't lasting punishment—one isn't put in a concentration camp—one isn't sent to Siberia, but it does make you more scared), and the whole thing about writing is to be free, unimpeded, to let the unconscious flow. It didn't stop me, though, and I'm rather proud of that.

Do you think that the presence of censorship spurred you on to creativity in any way?

Not at all. It's a premise that many people put forward. How an obstacle, a handicap, and so on, can be a spur. I think that's nonsense. I think the need to write and the wish to write and the dedication to write is a deep, complex, psychological urge and is there long before one cuts one's first tooth. These later obstacles are just irritations. The inner urge is to do, I think, with an abiding dissatisfaction; a kind of grief with life. Any writers I admire, I feel that in their work—that unassuageable pain.

The Irish Writer in Exile

You once said that Ireland was a very difficult place for you as a writer, and it wasn't just because of censorship.[2]

Well, there's the official censorship, and there's the everyday censorship.

What's that?

It's the people in the town or village where you might happen to live, being very aware of your comings and goings, your movements, and your possible writing. Writing itself is hard enough besides putting up with personal stick about it. It irks me, people constantly saying to me, "Oh, why don't you come back to Ireland," as if living elsewhere were a kind of betrayal. Well, T. S. Eliot was an American who lived in England, and Samuel Beckett is an Irishman who lives in Paris—so what?

Do you think that Irish people still have that attitude toward the writer?

Yes, they can be at once possessive and quite scornful. Most Irish people secretly, or not so secretly, have a desire to write. Dublin being a great example of it—scores of unwritten novels. Many say, "Oh, well, I could do that—I could write what she does."

Do you think that the position of women in Ireland makes it that bit more difficult for the woman writer?

It does because she's not supposed to write. (*A*) she's supposed to keep her thoughts to herself. And (*B*) she's supposed to be doing maternal, domestic, useful things; not things that are the provenance of a man.

You said once that you felt the Irish church wanted women to be almost inhuman.[3]

Did I use the word "inhuman"?

You did. Is that too strong?

It is inaccurate. I think, wanted to keep them frozen—mute.

What kind of image of women do you think people wish to see in Ireland?

The pedestal image: devoid of sexual desires, maternal, devout, attractive. Quite a handful!

Do you think that one of the things that upset people about you as a writer was that you failed to present that image?

Probably. I offended several fashions. I offended the Catholic church. I betrayed Irish womanhood. They even used that phrase —I was a "smear on Irish womanhood." I betrayed my own community by writing about their world. I showed two Irish girls full of yearnings and desires. Wicked!

Ireland is a country which is familial and communal. Do you think Irish people resent the writer, and particularly the woman writer, when she steps outside that community and asks for the freedom to write?

Yes, I think so, because it seems such a scandalous thing to do. It's a rebellion.

Ireland Today

Do you think that censorship continues to be a threat in Ireland today?

Not as many books are now banned, but we have to take into account the prevailing social climate. Banning is only the tip of the iceberg. Keeping our psyches closed is the main bogey.

Alas, I don't feel that there is much passion for literature in Ireland now. It's on the wane. It's "Dynasty" and the potboilers, and that's sad. Very sad, really. They should be devouring the great classics—Thackeray, Dickens, Joyce, Proust, Flaubert, Chekov, and most of all Shakespeare, the greatest poet and psychologist of all.

What kind of damage do you think censorship has done in Ireland?

Closed the minds of people. Frightened them. It's a fuckup, if you'll excuse the word. Ignorance and darkness and bigotry only lead to psychic sickness.

Who do you think is responsible for this damage?

The church. It's the church and the blind adherence of people—the Faithful.

What was your attitude toward the result of the 1983 Abortion Referendum, which effectively ensured that abortion is illegal in Ireland?

I was horrified. I couldn't believe it. I was in Ireland at the time when the debates were going on, and I saw a lot of those television debates and went to some meetings. I thought it was a step back, far back. No woman is overjoyed to have an abortion but if she must have it, she should not be made to feel like a criminal. It's a serious and traumatic thing for a woman, and she needs support, not cudgels.

There has been a recent decision in the Supreme Court in favour of the Society for the Protection of the Unborn Child which refuses women access to information on abortion. What would be your response to that decision?

It's tragic. Little do they know it's also a potential form of murder. Murder to the lives of women who are already born and trying to live their lives. The zealots never take into account the penalizing due to poverty and exhaustion that arises from having large families—the unhappiness for the mother, the damage that redounds on the children. They don't take that into account. I don't think much of Pope John Paul II's opinions; he may be a charming man and a great traveller, but he's a dogmatist. Women's lot is hard anywhere, but an Irishwoman's lot is ten times harder.

Why do you say her lot is ten times harder?

The reasons we have just discussed: fear binds and imprisons. Also Irish men do not give their wives the kind of companionship that matters. Many Irish women are still in fear and trembling of their men. I spend a lot of time in America, and there it's almost reversed. American men are terrified of their wives. American women are so much more predatory. I don't recommend that either. Balance is all; the balance that comes through a mutual under-standing, which in turn comes from education. Education is not statistics or computers; it's knowledge and self-knowledge. A bit of Buddhism would do this country a power of good.

About a year ago Alex Comfort's sex manual, *The Joy of Sex,* was banned for the second time. What is your response to the banning of that book?

Was it because of the photographs?

Apparently it was the bondage section.

Well, "there's more kinds of bondage than one" would be my last word on censorship!

The Principle of Censorship

What is your attitude toward censorship as a matter of prin-ciple?

On grounds of morality, I think it's absurd. There's some junk writ-ten which is also immoral. There is as well a kind of panoply of ignorance about literature. Rubbish fills the bookshelves, but no one cares about that. Let's up the standard of literature; let's burn your typical titivating, slushy, cretinous, manipulative best seller. These things are the harm; they foul the mind.

You once said that you felt censorship was rooted in fear.[4] What kind of fear?

Fear of knowledge. Fear of communicating our desires, our secrets, our stream of consciousness.

Do you think that kind of fear lies behind censorship in Ireland?

It lies behind censorship everywhere—Ireland, South Africa, Russia. The Russians know it better than anyone, by putting their poets in exile, in labour camps, or killing them all off. It's a fear that things will get out of hand. It's a fear that thinking and openness will spread. Now the Russians and the Irish differ radically in their opinion of what is to be banned or what is censorable. The Russian censorship has always been political, and the Irish has always been religious. Sex is the factor here. The fear would be that the people would become libidinous, rampant. This makes me sad, really sad. Repression and ignorance is the biggest rot of all because from it springs sickness, insanity, schizophrenia, which as we know is very high in Ireland. By saying "Thou shalt not," one opens the sluice gates to inner dilemma.

L E E D U N N E

Lee Dunne was born in Dublin in 1934. In the 1970s virtually all of his novels were banned by the Irish Censorship
Board. His novel *The Cabfather,* the last Irish novel banned
in Ireland, was not unbanned until 1988. Ironically, two
other novels that he wrote under the pseudonym Peter
O'Neill for the Olympia Press, *Hell Is Filling Up* and *The
Corpse Wore White,* were never banned. Since the publication of his first novel, *Goodbye to the Hill,* in 1965,
Dunne has been a well-known figure in Ireland. He has
written extensively for television and radio, including the
first 750 episodes of the popular serial "Harbour Hotel,"
and has hosted his own television show. He currently lives
in County Wicklow. He was interviewed by Julia Carlson
for Article 19 in Galway on 5 November 1987.

The Personal Experience
of Censorship

**You were effectively singled out by the Censorship Board in
the 1970s when a great number of your books were banned.
Do you have any idea why that might have happened?**

I called the head of the Censorship Board a cretin on television,
and it was put to me, Your next book's going to get the hammer.
That was *Paddy Maguire Is Dead.* He was mumbling, waffling politically, on the television, and I said, "Will you answer the questions!
You're mumbling. Are you a cretin? What is the story? Why are you
here?" We were guests on a television programme, and the whole
thing of censorship came up. You see, I had advocated birth control
in this country in 1968 on television. I said, "If there were birth
control allowed, one in three of the illegitimate children being born
in London today wouldn't be from Irish girls." I said, "Somebody
around here is getting laid. These are not immaculate conceptions."
I said all those things, so I was a target. When I saw Gay Byrne
showing them how to use a contraceptive on television recently—
I said all that in '68. No wonder they thought I was nuts because
Gay was maligned for that. No wonder they thought I was the devil
in 1968. I guess the cumulative effect of all of that was inevitably
the banning.

**When you began to write, were you at all conscious of the
fact that your books might be banned?**

No. Hutchinson published *Goodbye to the Hill.* I got an approbation
from them three days after I gave them the manuscript. I thought
I wouldn't hear from them for six months, and they wanted it immediately. I was thrilled, but prior to that a man called Frederick
Warburg of Secker and Warburg in London said, "Excellent. You
have the stuff of great writing in you, but I won't publish this because an Irish sale would be important, and I feel this book would
be banned in Ireland." We're talking 1964.

Goodbye to the Hill **wasn't banned, though.**

I had the picture banned. We made a movie of *Goodbye to the Hill*, a Hollywood movie called *Paddy,* a rather lyrical—not a great film, a nice movie. There was a scene of Maureen Toal getting into bed with Des Cave, an Irish actress and an Irish guy. They're going to make love: they get into bed, they embrace, and you cut. The film was banned. There was nothing else. That was shown in 1970 precisely. It was made in 1968. It was a charming little movie that wasn't going to hurt anybody, and it was banned. To see a nice movie made in Ireland with an Irish crew, Irish stars, written by an Irish writer, to see a film like that banned—I felt really sad. It was a joke when you can see *Rambo* and all that. This was just a picture about a kid who was scared and hungry and frightened and promiscuous and just looking for somewhere to be warm and this woman who had a need. They hadn't banned the novel, no. I think the novel rather took them by surprise. At the time it caused a sensation.

Was there controversy over the play of *Goodbye to the Hill,* **too?**

In 1978 I had a leading newspaper critic walk out of the play *Goodbye to the Hill* at the Eblana saying goodbye to Lee Dunne. He was offended by what went on on the stage, and it really is a very funny, very touching, very honest kind of play. The boy questions God in a very overt manner. His mother tells him his younger brother is dying of tuberculosis in the fifties, and he says, "Is there anything we can do?" She says, "There's nothing we can do." She says, "Sometimes it's very hard to understand, very hard to accept God's will." Boy furious, turns and says, "God's will. God in his almighty mercy. Jesus help us all if he ever loses his fucking temper!" And there's a pause in the theatre, and the place explodes. But the juxtaposition of God and the word "fuck" threw the critic.

It was on in the Olympia for eight weeks in '85 and did terrific business. The producer had been apprehensive. He wanted to change, say, the word "tits" to the word "breast." I said, "Well, Harry would never say 'breast.' Harry would sneer at someone who would say 'breast.' Can you not see he's a male chauvinist pig of all time, and he thinks in those terms? I couldn't write that because he won't say that."

There was still that kind of concern about diction in 1985?

In '85. The producer, a wonderful man, just worried it would offend. And you can go in and buy Jackie Collins's *Hollywood Wives.* Have you read it? Dear, oh dear. She's wicked.

Were you ever subjected to unofficial censorship of any other kind?

I had a column in the *Evening Herald,* and I wrote a couple of articles that were fine. I wrote another article called "I Am an Alcoholic" to say to people: "Don't be frightened; it's OK to be an alkie if you stop drinking." I got great praise for this. Then I wrote an article called "Goodbye to the Pill," questioning the pope's right to say no, after the whole hierarchy in and out of the church, Catholic laymen and clerics, had actually spoken in favour of birth control. I said, "If the prime minister of this country had a referendum and we voted yes, we would question his sanity. Why can't we do this with the pope?" I lost the newspaper column. One day the editor of the paper was saying to me, "We'll harness your talent." I'll never forget the phrase. Three weeks later the guy said, "I can't run the column; we have an abundance of features." If I were doing it again, I'd go a slightly different route. I would not lose my argument because of the manner in which I presented it.

Later, on Irish radio at lunchtime I got the word "abortion" on the air. What one had to do was to set it up in such a way that over a period of three weeks—by the time you said the word— the audience knew exactly what you were talking about, and they all felt wonderful and nobody complained. In other words, you had Noreen saying, "You won't believe what he asked me to do when he came to London with me." And somebody says, "Well, tell me." And you cut. Somebody else in a scene later says, "No wonder Noreen slapped his face. How could he suggest such a thing to a girl like that?" You spin it out, and when he finally says, "You mean he asked her to have an abortion," everybody knows and everybody's delighted that they're right, so there were no complaints. I'd have done that with the articles I bludgeoned my way through, in the interests of continuing.

Paddy Maguire Is Dead was the first of your novels to be banned. How did you feel when that happened?

I did mind that being banned. It's not a great novel, but there's much good in it. It was about an alcoholic. It was about basically my own experiences. Guys came to me and said, "It helped me more than three years of AA." Truly. And yes, there's sex in the book, but sex arose out of the alcoholic's desperate need for somewhere to hide. It's not about sex; it's about insecurity. Any intelligent human being knows that, but those people regarded it as sex.

The book was defended vociferously by the writers Francis Stuart and John Broderick. John Broderick actually said, "It is criminal that people can have the power to ban such a book." Mary Manning, a very well known critic, said that the book was almost boringly moral.

I wrote that book with a good intention, with a good heart, and I fought to have that book printed directly into paperback. I was a hardback writer, and I wanted the ordinary person to be able to purchase it on the same day as people who could afford a hardback book: a kind of idealistic notion which was tantamount to just digging a hole and burying my career because you don't get the same review possibilities. I have no regrets about that, but I was very angry.

Did you feel the same way when the cabbie books were banned?

I didn't mind them banning the cabbie books because they weren't very good. I had six books come out in a year. These publishers had this notion that these funny, sexy books would sell, and, indeed, they sold like hot cakes in England. I wrote them quickly. I wrote all those taxi books in ten days each because the money was good, and they just wanted them very quickly. They didn't want them good; they just wanted them Thursday. Train-ride books.

They were funny, sexy books. Now, by definition, a funny book is not obscene.

What were the books about?

Those little books, those cabbie books, were like cowboy books, not as good as Zane Grey, but as good as some of those westerns that creep around from time to time. That's what they were like.

They were about a team of randy cabdrivers in England that were more interested in getting laid than in making money on the cab. But they were funny guys. They were characters. Their whole attitude to life was infantile, which the narrator of the book—I wrote them first-person singular—is very aware of. Essentially books for men because the descriptions of women perhaps would be patronizing and very sexist and all that, but that's the kind of guy I was. That's the kind of people that were in the books. They had titles like *Midnight Cabbie, The Cabfather,* and *The Cabbie Who Came in from the Cold.* John Le Carré was thrilled; he thought it was great fun. Funny books, by definition. And they are funny, if you make allowances for the people in them. They were banned en bloc.

***Maggie's Story* is a more serious novel than the cabbie books. But it was banned, too, wasn't it?**

Before it got hit people bought it, and women came up to me because they understood. It's about a woman who got married in love and found that her husband could not get it together sexually. All she ever wanted out of life was a family. She'd had a couple of affairs premarriage, and she couldn't tell him about that because he was that kind of a guy. She couldn't help him sexually. She couldn't put her hand on him in bed, or he would think she was a whore—that kind of mentality. She was a rather wonderful, lovely woman, so she finally gets somebody to give her a child. She does that four times, I think. I got into her head. I got into Maggie's head. I found overall terrific approbation from ordinary people, working-class people, because they're my people.

Were you ever angry enough to protest or take any kind of a stand against censorship?

I got one hundred copies of *Paddy Maguire Is Dead* after it was banned, and I stood at the top of Grafton Street wearing a placard saying "Paddy Maguire Is Alive and Well and Living in Dublin." I gave those books away very slowly, signing them in an effort to be arrested. Two policemen stood by and never came near me. The papers came and took pictures of me and interviewed me on the spot. There was no reaction from the two policemen standing there. It was as though they were there to ensure I didn't get arrested in case somebody else came along and made a mistake. I created what you might call a public disturbance. I broke the law by giving them away. I gave them away, by the way, rather than sell them because I didn't want to be arrested for breaking a street law, not having a peddler's license. I didn't want them to be able to summons me for breaking a local bylaw. I wanted a much larger scale. That was a big thing to do. That was bigger than writing to a newspaper or an article for a magazine. I was prepared to go to court. I was prepared to be taken away. I was prepared to spend time overnight in jail if necessary. And it failed miserably.

Why do you think it failed? Do you think it was because they didn't want the publicity?

That's right, that's right. They didn't want to risk the publicity.

Did you get support from other writers in your protest?

I'm not going to name names, but I wrote to a lot of writers telling them I was going to make this protest, and not one person joined me. Afterwards, when I got to meet them and told them, they certainly backed me up, and I don't doubt that had they been available at the time they might have showed up for me. But there were a lot of people who didn't show—did not answer my letter.

Are you bitter about that?

Not at all. No, honest. On the live-and-let-live thing, people have to do what's right for them.

Did you ever make another protest against censorship?

No, I didn't. I just didn't bother. I thought the hell with it; I've done what I could do. I wasn't angry enough to take it further, to make a federal case out of it.

Did you ever think about leaving Ireland because your books had been banned?

Up to 1969 I was living in England, and I really never expected to live in Ireland again. Then my marriage broke up in England, and I came home. I just quit drinking. It was 1969. When I came home I saw this country that I'd never really seen before because in my youth here I was so angry. I was angry at being poor. I was angry at not having money to buy the books I wanted to read, no money to go to the theatre. I was angry at the way there had been a kind of snob thing created in this country. You couldn't really be a writer unless you'd been to Trinity. You really weren't entitled to go to the Abbey or the Gate if you didn't wear certain clothes, so I was angry, and I didn't really see this country. I came back and I just fell in love with Ireland. During the last twenty years I spent almost three years living in Manhattan being very close to a Broadway production for my play. And when I came home, I promised myself that I would never be out of Ireland voluntarily for more than six weeks. I would be happy to live and die in County Wicklow. I love Ireland. I love the Irish. I'm very happy.

Censorship and Class

You were one of the first writers after Sean O'Casey and Brendan Behan, who also were banned, to give a voice to the Dublin working class.

Yes, that's why *Goodbye to the Hill* took people by surprise—because everybody knew they could write this book, but they didn't. In my innocence I didn't even realize what I was doing. That book attacked the system—the way in which I had seen politicians come to our slum and shake hands with people and barely conceal the distaste they felt, while they made sycophantic remarks to poverty-stricken people in the hope that these people would go and vote for them, and you never saw them again, et cetera, et cetera. The power of the church—it's all attacked in *Goodbye to the Hill*. A lot of people who were against the sex in it were in favour of the effort I made to say, "Take a look at what's happening here." The same thing with *Paddy Maguire Is Dead*—I really went for the jugular in many ways.

Do you think that the decisions of the Censorship Board represent the attitudes of the working class?

The people on the Censorship Board are all members of that same upper middle class.[1] It's really a tiny minority of privileged people. They don't have any Dublin carpenter; they don't have any road sweeper from the Dublin Corporation, and plenty of them read. They don't have any housewife who works in a factory and has a library card. If there's a housewife on the Censorship Board, she'll be a housewife in name only. She'll have somebody doing the washing up and cleaning the house. She'll drive her own car. The common man had no voice, and as a common man writing in the voice of common people, I had no representation on the board. It shows you: if you're rocking the boat, you're rocking the system's boat, and if the people viewing that are of the system, they're going to stop you. There's no mix on the board. It's OK to have a nun if you have an atheist. They're holding up a corner of the establishment. The establishment's need to opt for respectability in lieu of honesty is a mistake. Oh, what a mistake. To opt for peace in lieu of freedom: mistake.

You mentioned earlier that you fought to have *Paddy Maguire Is Dead* printed directly into paperback. Do you think that hardback books were getting by the censors in the seventies when paperbacks weren't?

Yes. In the same way, when I was a kid, they built these awful blocks of flats for the poor, and there was no tree; there was no blade of grass because we were poor. It never occurred to anybody that we might have any modicum, sliver, of aesthetic sense. We didn't need trees. Whereas today the Dublin Corporation are building wonderful houses with gardens, with shrubbery, with trees. It's wonderful. I wrote about it recently in the papers, praising them for the fact that they'd become aware that poor people, too, can have a need for beauty in their immediate surroundings. I do feel that Ireland was always like that—very patronizing to the poor. The Gate Theatre mentality: boiled shirtfronts for first nights.

If you get a book published in hardback and it costs seven pounds, it can be published. If it's published for a pound, it will be banned. It's OK for the elite who can afford the seven pounds, but it's not OK for Joe Soap who can afford a pound.[2] So in a way censorship is dishonest. I fought with those people. I said, "If *Paddy Maguire Is Dead* was published in hardback, this book wouldn't be banned. You're creating a kind of economic morality. A book that is clean at five pounds is dirty at fifty pence." I was very angry.

Do you think that kind of hypocrisy is characteristic of Irish society?

Ireland's a kind of country where if you have a series in *Sunday World,* very few people mention it to you, but if you have three articles in the *Irish Times,* everybody you meet says it was a wonderful series. It's that kind of country in many ways. Everybody buys the *Sunday World.* It's the first paper to sell, but nobody actually admits to reading it. What's wrong with reading the *Sunday World* if you want to? Nothing. What's wrong with having a girl inside if somebody wants to look at it and if the housewife derives a little benefit that night from the fact that he's thinking about a twenty-two-year-old with big jugs? Who cares—if he looks after her, if she's getting her conjugals? Who cares?

Would you say, then, that a craving for middle-class respectability lies behind Irish censorship?

I think it stems from shame, shame relating to sex, guilt relating to sex, fear relating to sex. Censorship was engendered in us on a personal level—"Don't let people know your business." The Irish are wonderful, wonderful people who deserve a better kind of script.

At sixteen, I was expected to ask a girl out. I was expected to decide where to take her. I was expected to take the lead in everything, and I didn't know what time it was. So I had to develop a character. Nobody said, "Be real"; they said, "Be nice." I developed a personality and so did my contemporaries. The girl was told that she had a certain role to play and she played it. Those people sometimes married. Can you think of anything more awful than that? There was no shared reality in any of their courting, and nobody was there to enlighten them. Nobody listened. They didn't want to hear truth. We're talking about a time when the word "communication," as we use it today, hadn't even been coined.

You mentioned a script. Who would you say wrote that script?

There's no question that the power of the church has been too great and remains so. I will be maligned for saying this, but that's how I feel. I really think that the whole thing needs to be looked at. It's about control rather than about love in my opinion. It's like going back to the thing of no flowers in the slum—"It doesn't matter; we'll make the decision." The church does the same thing in many ways.

Ireland Today

Would you comment on the current activity of the Censorship Board—its recent banning of books such as *The Joy of Sex*.

It's a joke, a sick joke, to ban those books. To ban *The Joy of Sex*—the very word "joy" is enough to get it banned. We're still living in a society where you're not supposed to enjoy yourself. The Irish will take lessons to drive a car or ride a horse, but we're all supposed to be divinely inspired to be lovers. Total nonsense. To openly admit that sex is wonderful and that it can be joyous and beautiful and affirming is really regarded with a great deal of suspicion, distaste, and repugnance by a great deal of our society which is still locked into that idea of respectability. The lights-out syndrome.

Do you think that the church still wields the same degree of power over people in Ireland that it did before?

I don't think there's any doubt about it. The younger generation are not buying the deal in the way we did, and I praise them for that. There's more criticism from the younger generation than from my generation or from the people who preceded me. *In Dublin* magazine is very healthy. *The Phoenix.* I think they're healthier despite anything that's said against the present twenty- to twenty-five-year-olds. I think they're the healthiest people we've ever produced. I love them for saying, "No, I don't buy this at all."

Why do you think censorship has managed to exist for so long in Ireland?

I think the fear of change is endemic in Irish society. People become relatively comfortable in uncomfortable situations, settling for less than they are worth. A woman should be able to say to her husband, "I'd like to do this" or "I'd like to do that," without him thinking, "My God, where did you get such a notion—you're my wife—you shouldn't think like that."

That freedom still doesn't exist?

Oh, I don't think it does at all. We were brought up in a society where if a girl wasn't a virgin, she wasn't a good girl—this kind of nonsense. It exists to a great extent today. It's very out-of-date. It's very sad. Very real.

I'm astonished by how parochial at times the Irish situation is. I was doing a radio programme some months ago in Bray on the twenty-first birthday publication of *Goodbye to the Hill.* This young eighteen-year-old guy read my book, and he said, "It's a great book, but it's a dirty book." I was astonished to find there are still people who think like that.

The Principle of Censorship

What is your attitude toward censorship as a matter of principle?

On a yes-or-no basis, I'm against it as a matter of principle, but with obvious caveats. I do think that you have to protect children. I do think that pornographic magazines, et cetera, et cetera, should be kept out of the reach of children. I would say to you, "You can go into this establishment that should be there in town, and you can buy them without being embarrassed or having any shame or any of the rest of it." It's not for me to say that somebody's sick or somebody's perverted or whatever. I have no right. I feel that very strongly.

You're the only Irish writer whose books are still banned today. How do you feel about that?

It means very little to me personally, but I think it's a shame that this kind of thing exists in the world. This town is full of pubs, and I don't have to buy a drink. I really think we add to our civilization by admitting that certain people have certain needs.

There should be organized government brothels in the country. We put them in a certain place, and we have doctors checking out the girls every week. There are no pimps beating people up or making money out of this. But we're too respectable to make money from that kind of thing; yet we will make a million pounds a day from alcohol, which is killing the nation, or we will make it from cigarettes. To say to people, "That's there for you. If that's what you need, go. Don't tell us afterwards you didn't know where you were. We are setting it up like Clery's department store. It's a block in O'Connell Street, and you can get what you want in there, and you'll be safe. You won't be robbed. You won't be beaten up. You won't be blackmailed because you went in and had a massage." Let us create some freedom for people who've got hang-ups. On a yes-or-no basis, I'm against abortion, but it's up to the woman to decide. I have no right to tell her, "We have made a decision for you." But they still think I'm nuts. Basically, a lot of people think this, but they will not say it.

I'm a Christian. I believe in Christ. I'm not an organized Christian; I'm not part of anything; but I believe in Christ. I believe in love, love as he showed us how to love. I don't think he would approve of us punishing people who are in any way inadequate, in any way hung-up, because Christ says, "I love you, buddy." He doesn't say, "I love you if you're strong and respectable and only go with your wife or whatever." He just said, "I love you." That's the difference in the love that Jesus talked about and the thing they call love today in our society.

MAURICE LEITCH

Maurice Leitch was born in Muckamore, County Antrim, in 1933 and is the only writer interviewed here to come from a Protestant background. Two of his novels were banned in Southern Ireland—*Liberty Lad* (1965) and *Poor Lazarus* (1969), which won the *Guardian* Fiction Prize. Both novels are highly critical of the Northern Protestant community and deal with the subject of homosexuality. Leitch left Northern Ireland in 1970 and now lives in London, where he worked for the BBC until 1988. His recent fiction includes *Chinese Whispers* (1987) and *Burning Bridges* (1989). He was interviewed by Julia Carlson for Article 19 in London on 25 June 1987.

The Personal Experience
of Censorship

How aware were you of Irish literary censorship as a writer in the North?

I knew about it, and there was always talk. The most notorious cases were John McGahern and Edna O'Brien. In the North of Ireland where I grew up, we knew there was something called the [Roman] Index, and we knew there was a list. If I had come from a Catholic background, I probably would have known that list, but coming from a Protestant background, I didn't know it. I just read the books that I liked; I didn't pick them out because there might have been a salacious content or something like that. I remember we all had to read *Lady Chatterley's Lover.* That was the other censorship thing, and that was the book everybody read for kicks.

When you began to write were you at all aware of censorship as something that might affect you personally?

Not in a personal way, I wasn't aware of censorship. I think the basic reason for that was at that particular period—and I think it still exists to this day—my natural focus or target was London, like a lot of writers from the North of Ireland. I never really thought of being published in Dublin.

How do you feel now about the fact that your books were banned in the Irish Republic?

I have to tell you now that I'm very pleased in a way. I think that makes my two books much stronger in many ways. I think that means that they were hard-hitting and powerful and honest, those three adjectives, if they were banned. I think if a novelist was writing at that particular time about what was going on in his environment, if he was youngish and wasn't banned, there was something wrong somewhere because he was closing his eyes to what was going on around him.

Most of the banned writers in the Republic were harassed in various ways because of the content of their books. Did that ever happen to you?

I did get a lot of backlash, particularly my first book. Nothing to do with the job. I'm talking socially, not from my own immediate family, but from people who knew me socially and from the village I came from. It still affects certain people. It seemed terribly shocking that I would actually mention the fact that homosexuality existed, particularly in an Irish context, whether North or South, because there's not much difference really between the attitudes North or South. It just seemed a subject worthy of writing about because it was another extension of repression. Ireland is sexually repressed; let's face it. It was also part of the fifties and sixties; that sort of repression was everywhere almost.

How did you feel when people responded to your work in that way?

Well, I was very shocked. I was very innocent. Like most writers writing their first novel, I was writing the way I felt and very strongly. But I was very surprised by the response when it came out. My books still—this sounds like self-pity—get a dusty reception in the North, but I think that's very natural. I think the majority of Irish writers are always given a very bad time in their own homeland.

The kind of sexuality you describe in the novels, the stunted, twisted sexuality, do you think that's a particularly Irish problem?

Yes, there's no doubt about that. It's a fear of the sensual almost in any shape or form, which obviously comes from the church whether it's the Protestant tradition or the repressive Catholic tradition. There's no doubt about that.

So you think it crosses the divide?

We've got that in common. That's one reason why the border might disappear—about the only reason, I would imagine.

You mentioned that people were shocked by the homosexual content of *The Liberty Lad*. Did they fix upon it, in particular, as being offensive?

Yes. Also they thought that it was untrue: they felt I was doing this deliberately to create sales for my books. Some reviewers in the North said that about my last book, *Silver's City* [1981]. I remember very well how shattered I was. The first review I read was in Belfast. This man gave me the worst review I've ever had. He said that the book was a disgrace: it was a disgusting book; it wallowed in filth—all sorts of things like that. I was quite shattered. Then, of course, I went back to London, and suddenly I realized that the reviews here were ecstatic, and I won the Whitbread Prize. But he was saying what they said about the first book. What he was really saying was, You've no right to put us in this light; what will other people think of us?

Was the political content of your books attacked in the same way as the sexual content was attacked?

At that particular time somehow Unionist MPs were fair game, still are, I think. In *Poor Lazarus* people didn't like the way I wrote about the Orangemen, and in my last book a lot of people didn't like the way I wrote about the Protestant paramilitaries. Again, they thought that was biased, and I was trying to sensationalize the whole thing. What they were really saying about the last book was —I think in a funny way I've come full circle from the first book— that I set out deliberately to present a picture of Northern Ireland which would coincide with what the English felt about it. I was a traitor, a turncoat, which is one of the favourite epithets in Ireland. It's always been there. I think, in a way, that's what makes Irish writers write the way they do.

I remember when I was living in London—I left Northern Ireland in 1970—one night the phone rang about one in the morning, and this woman rang me from Northern Ireland. I don't know how she got my number. We had a long conversation. First thing she said was, "Why do you write about us like that? Why don't you write nice things about us for a change?" That was the most direct form of review, if you like, I've ever received. And we talked and talked. "Why do you put us in this awful light, particularly at this stage in our history when everyone seems to be attacking us?" That seems to be a recurring thing—that we don't want the outside world to see us in this bad light.

How did you respond to her?

I said to her, "Look, the reason why I write like this is because I love my country so much and so deeply, but I'm angry with it. I want to change it. If I didn't care, I wouldn't write like this." I'm on the soapbox, really. If you look at writers like John McGahern, Edna O'Brien, John Broderick, and Anthony West, we are all angry with injustice and repression, and we want to change it. It's not that we're saying, "A plague on all your houses"; we would just simply get on the next boat and start writing about England. The thing Irish writers find very difficult is to write about anything other than Ireland.

When you were living in the North, were you aware of unofficial censorship of any kind?

There's always social censorship—what you wear, what you say in company, things you don't want to do for fear of hurting your family. I think that's something terribly important. There's always that worry, that sort of battle. When I write this and my parents or my friends, close blood relatives, see this—you've got to take that risk. That's very difficult for an Irish writer because the family is such an important thing. It's very tribal.

Do you think that censorship influenced writers artistically, that it tempted them to shock or intimidated them into writing safe fiction?

I think it may have influenced a certain number of writers who put their own personal brakes on their material, perhaps the older generation who felt very strongly that they had to live and work in Ireland. I never really felt that. I wasn't under that pressure.

A writer I admire immensely is John Broderick. I think he went against the mainstream, but at the same time John Broderick came from a relatively privileged background. He could afford to do this sort of thing. The Irish have always been like that. They always allow people they think are different or more privileged than they are to get away with it. They're harder on their own kind. Someone like John McGahern or Edna O'Brien would get a much harder time than someone like John Broderick or, going earlier, someone from the ascendency class. That's one of the very cruel and ignoble aspects of Irish life.

Do you think censorship had the effect of radicalizing writers in any way, of radicalizing their art?

Yes, I think so; in that respect, it might be good for the writer and bad for the reader. It may have helped people like John McGahern and Edna O'Brien. At the same time, if you set out to write deliberately against the target and then at some stage that target, that barrier, is removed, it may be difficult for the artist to continue. It may be a way of thinking. Some writers do actually seem to keep circling back, to keep hitting the target, which may have disappeared. Some writers do keep harping along the same lines all the time—these repressions and so on. The repressions may have changed for the younger people. It's a fallout situation, isn't it? It's in the air all around you.

The Northern Writer in Exile

A significant number of writers from the North of Ireland have settled in the Republic. Did you ever consider living in Southern Ireland?

I went down to Dublin a lot and enjoyed it for short spells. I used to go to McDaid's and the pubs; I was working there for the BBC, doing recordings, and I made many good friends, but I didn't want to stay too long. All the jokes and stories about Dublin are perfectly true—people circling each other twenty-four hours a day, talking about the novels they're going to write. I think Dublin must be a deathtrap for any serious novelist.

Because of its incestuous quality?

Exactly. And the envy which is a peculiarly Irish thing—literary envy is something it seems they've invented and brought to its finest flowering. Novelists need a lot of time by themselves free from distractions and from anything that would dent their morale, which is not the strongest anyway. They didn't see me as any competition in a way; I was that strange figure from the North. We know quite well there's a divided nation there. The thing that I always noticed about the South, the writers in the South weren't interested in anything north of the border in cultural terms or any other terms, which I always thought was quite amazing. I can understand your ordinary man in the street not thinking about the North unless it's politically expedient, but I was surprised that the artists just had never been north and were quite content to make statements about the North but had never travelled north of Dundalk and had no intention of doing it. I think that still exists. It's breaking down a bit because quite a few have come up to the North and poked around a little bit—forgive me if I sound bitter—as if they were going into the outback and were looking at the natives, these strange people who dress up and wear funny costumes on the twelfth of July.

The movement really has always been the other way, hasn't it, from north to south?

The movement has always been that way. You talk to any person in the North, and I guarantee you that ninety-five percent have been at some stage in the South. We always went for holidays in the South of Ireland; Dublin was always a very exciting city to visit. Some people even remember going down there during the war years and being able to buy ice cream and things of that nature. We always felt that way, but the traffic doesn't come the other way.

Do you think the Northern writer is quite isolated, then?

Yes, but his sights are set on Britain: he looks out.

But how many people from Britain look to the North?

This was what Paul Theroux wrote in that travel book he did about going around Great Britain [The Kingdom by the Sea]. He said in the book that he had never once met anyone who had been to the North of Ireland. I suppose people in the North do feel very isolated and very frenzied—that they have to create their own culture and history themselves. I think that's why there's been such an outburst of writing talent in the North. It's slightly unbalanced when you think of poetry: all the great emphasis seems to be coming from the North. Perhaps it's because young writers in the South are somehow being put into the shade in comparison with Longley and Muldoon and Simmons and Heaney and Paulin. It seems strangely unbalanced.

The idea of a literary tradition is something that has created a lot of problems, both emotionally and intellectually, for writers from the North. Has that been true for you?

I don't think there's much tradition, really, in the North. There've been sporadic bits of writing, but no real tradition. There's a strongish theatre tradition in the North. It wasn't as strong as the Abbey Theatre, but they did have their own Ulster Literary Theatre, which died out a bit, but it's beginning to reappear again with people like Stewart Parker and Brian Friel.

The people I modelled myself on were Hemingway, F. Scott Fitzgerald, Faulkner. Faulkner particularly. Then later I discovered Flannery O'Connor and Eudora Welty, people like that. They seemed to be writing from a similar background to mine.

So you never identified with the literary tradition of the Republic in any way?

I admired the short story writers, O'Connor, O'Faolain, and I admired John McGahern very intensely and Edna O'Brien and Broderick. I read them, but I felt I had more in common with American writers or even some British writers, provincial writers like Sillitoe, angry young men. I thought I was in that same tradition, particularly in *Saturday Night and Sunday Morning*. My first book was based in a mill village in the North, which is not typically Irish. I mean, they don't have any industrial experience in the South. The environment I came from in the North was totally different, and I wasn't going to write about farmers and fisherfolk and people drinking themselves to death in Dublin pubs. I just said, I'm not interested in those themes because I thought it was all sort of therapy steeped in the past.

The sort of writer they want to be in Ireland is a writer in the same pattern as all the writers who went before. The thing about the Catholic writing tradition, which I think is a basic fault in many ways, is that there's no real revolutionary attitude to writing. What they feel is they must put another little stone on top of the cairn instead of knocking the cairn down as Joyce did. The majority of writers—they are conservative. They're Catholic in their way of thinking, and they don't really want to damage the status quo too much. I think that's very much part of most writers, even a writer like Seamus Heaney whom I admire immensely. We've never really talked about this, but I feel this strongly in his work. His work fits inside constraints because of his tribal background. Whereas a Protestant writer doesn't have these constraints because, in a curious way, it's a natural thing for the Protestant writer to protest, as it were. It's a long tradition.

You said earlier that you thought most Irish writers were given a bad time at home. Why do you think that's true?

I think it's something to do with the Irish mentality, the provincialism of Ireland. They have inbuilt safeguards to prevent anyone from challenging the herd or tribal instinct. If anyone gives the impression, even in the slightest way, that he or she might be wanting to do something different, immediately the walls go up. That's very strongly apparent in Ireland, North or South. At the same time, I have to counter that by saying provincialism anywhere is like that. I think it's very difficult for a writer today coming from the North.

Everyone is looking very, very carefully that you don't rock the boat too much, and you don't give a bad impression. I'm sure this exists in some degree in the South, but not to such a great degree.

Do you think that there's often an effort to repress the individual in the Irish community?

Yes. It's there for obvious reasons. Anything that damages the tribal fabric is dangerous. The church, whether it's Protestant or Catholic, that's the way they work—to keep people on a level so they're more easily controlled. I think anyone in Ireland who stands up and puts forward unpalatable truths—about basically a peasant community, North and South—is always in danger of being maligned, called turncoat or traitor.

The Principle of Censorship

You said earlier that the Irish writer who wasn't banned was closing his eyes to what was going on around him. Do you think that was what Irish censorship was all about—closing the eyes of the Irish people to what was going on around them?

I think that's what censorship is: censorship is trying to protect people from the realities of their life. I think also they didn't want the outside world to look at the country in a negative way. The people who go in for censorship, at the end of the day, haven't thought it out very much, have they? I have utter contempt for them. I think most writers have.

What is your attitude toward censorship as a matter of principle?

I'm opposed to any form of censorship. Well, pornography—you come up against pornography. I don't know what you say to that one. I think there is a certain type of pornography which should be banned, but who's going to do the banning? That's the difficult thing. I think there are certain books that are damaging, things that would damage children and people's attitude to children. I think in a curious way violent books are much more dangerous than sexual books—books, movies which extoll violence. Like the *Rambo* films. Violent rapes of women. They should be banned, but who's going to do it? How do you control it? There has to be some form of control over them. I take a selfish view. If it's well written, if it's beautifully written—I'm prepared to believe that if it's art, it doesn't damage.

In general, what do you think the attitude of the Northern Protestant community is toward censorship as a matter of principle?

I think if you took a head count today in the North of Ireland, just as many people would want censorship as in the South. Exactly the same. They would say, "Yes, there are certain things one shouldn't write about. We don't want that filth in our libraries." If the powers that be in Northern Ireland could have their way, they would have imposed censorship because the Unionists believe in censorship—religious censorship, sexual censorship, literary censorship. There's no difference whatsoever between the repressive religious ideologies.

BRIAN MOORE

Brian Moore was born in 1921 in Belfast, where his father
was a doctor. His first four novels were banned by the
Irish Censorship Board: *Judith Hearne* (1955, later banned
under the new title *The Lonely Passion of Judith Hearne*),
The Feast of Lupercal (1957), *The Luck of Ginger Coffey*
(1960), and *An Answer from Limbo* (1962). Since 1943,
Moore has lived outside Ireland. He served abroad with the
British Ministry of War Transport during World War II and
with the United Nations Relief and Rehabilitation Administration Mission to Poland after the war. In 1948 he emi-
grated to Canada, where he wrote his first novel and became a Canadian citizen. Since that time, Moore has won
many international prizes and fellowships for his work, including a Guggenheim Fellowship, the James Tait Black
Award, and the Canadian Governor General's Award. Two
of his novels have been nominated for the Booker Prize. In
1959 he moved to the United States, where he now lives in
Malibu, California. His recent novels include *Cold Heaven*
(1983) and *The Colour of Blood* (1987). A film version of
The Lonely Passion of Judith Hearne was made in 1987. He
was interviewed by Julia Carlson for Article 19 in London
on 22 September 1987.

The Personal Experience
of Censorship

You grew up in Belfast, where you went to Catholic schools. Did you have any experience of censorship growing up?

I went to St. Malachy's, which was the only Catholic boarding school in Belfast at the time. It was a terrible school. I would say the most serious effect of censorship that I can think of in Ireland doesn't start with book banning: it started, in my day, with the books chosen by Catholic institutions. The Roman Index was mild compared to the Irish Index—Graham Greene was banned—so what chance did people have of getting a proper literary education? It also meant that very bad, trashy Irish writers, who'd never gone abroad but were making a living at home, were thought of as much better than they were. The censorship of books in schools, the lack of choice which existed, condemned you in many ways, I think, to a third-class education.

This type of censorship still exists not only in Ireland. It comes back again and again in the United States like a recurrent disease. The school boards start banning books—it's absolutely incredible how stupid some of these people are. It's not so much political censorship; it's moral, religious censorship; it's censorship by ignorance. In my day in Ireland it was said that if two old ladies went around to a library and said a book was dirty, it was withdrawn pending investigation and possible banning.

What did it actually mean to you in your own education?

In all my days at school I had never heard of T. S. Eliot. I hadn't read Joyce, Auden, Hemingway, any of the people who later influenced me, until I moved away from my Irish Catholic background and, at the beginning of the war, I went to work in the National Fire Service. There I met a man who was a Protestant, much older than I. He started talking about these books and I got them from

111

him. I wonder what would have happened to me if, at the age of seventeen, I hadn't met this man and hadn't been exposed to these writers. The whole modern movement was opened up to me by an outsider. I just didn't know anything about it. My father, who was a well-read man, hadn't read these people either and had been brainwashed into the notion that people such as Belloc and Chesterton were the greatest English writers of their day.

Would you say, then, that censorship was as severe in Ulster as it was in the Republic?

To be fair, it seemed worse in the Republic than in Ulster. There seemed to be more interest in serious English writing in Ulster than in Southern Ireland. Ireland was cocooned in a parochial thing where the admired writers were Yeats and Shaw only because they were Irish or people like Belloc and Baring who were English Catholics. But nobody read Wilde; Wilde was very persona non grata.

When I came back to Ireland after the war, I was very enthused about Joyce. I found that well-educated people in Dublin just hadn't read him. They were all talking about Myles na gCopaleen. More people knew Flann O'Brien than knew James Joyce, which amazed me. I love Flann O'Brien's work, so it's not that I'm putting him down. But Joyce was a major Irish writer whom no one knew. My father, who was a great reader, said to me once, "James Joyce is a sewer." He never read him, but that was the attitude. And my father was not a banning person, though he was very religious. When I was in school, I wrote an essay in which I quoted Bernard Shaw. The headmaster was furious. He was a priest. He said, "Who has you reading this trash?" I went home and told Daddy about this, and he stormed up to the school and gave them hell.

In addition to censorship of ideas, were you aware of other kinds of censorship or repression when you were growing up?

Everybody was repressed. My mother came from Donegal, and they were farming people. It was a different background to my

father's—they were more what we would call peasants, except you
don't use that word in Ireland. I was quite amazed when I went
up there as a little boy to realize that what the priests were worried about was that country people had a very strong sexual urge,
something which we didn't seem to have in the cities. There was
a lot more hanky-panky, and there would have been—without tremendous control—a lot more extramarital children and that sort of
thing. I think there's something tragic in that—that the real Irish
country people were very healthy, strong people sexually and were
kept down. I noticed those things as a child in Donegal. People
went off up the lane, and you knew what they were up to. You
didn't see that in the city. Boys and girls would go to dances and
disappear out of the dance hall. There was a terrible lot of beating up of people—"Leave my daughter alone." You saw it. You felt
there was something going on. Then, of course, country people
were dealing with animals. You saw bulls going to stud. You saw
all these things which you never saw in the city, and you realized
there was a difference.

**Your first novel, *Judith Hearne,* was banned in 1955. What
personal memory do you have of the banning of your books?**

What I remember personally about it is—I'm related to Eoin Mac-
Neill and to the MacNeill family in Dublin.[1] They knew Archbishop
McQuaid—he was a heavy-duty banner, and it was his say-so in the
fifties which books were put on the Irish Index. He mentioned it
to Maire MacNeill, one of my cousins. He said, "I know that boy's
connected to your family, and it's ridiculous that he would write
this sort of book." So those books were banned on the say-so of
McQuaid.

Would you have been pleased that your books were banned?

Yes, I thought it meant I must be OK.

**What kind of response did you get from people in Ireland
when your books were banned? Your family, for example,
how did it respond to your work?**

Relatives of mine—brothers and sisters, cousins—I know a lot of them thought these books were terrible.

Did they say that when your books were banned?

These are questions we didn't ask each other. They didn't want to embarrass me, and I didn't want to embarrass them. My mother made a wonderful comment. I asked her what she thought of my first novel which she had just read, and she said, "How would I know what I thought of it; I was far too busy making sure I wasn't in it." Nowadays they will tell me that they like this book or they like that book. One of my sisters is a nun in England; she's a headmistress, and she's very well educated, bright. I know that she would like a book like *Catholics,* and I know she was interested in *Black Robe,* too, and she will be interested in this book [*The Colour of Blood*], but I don't think she would have read those books if she hadn't known me. I don't think, although they're educated people, that any of the members of my family—my sisters or brothers, with the exception of my brother who lives in Canada, who's in a totally different world—would ever have read my books if they hadn't been written by their brother.

What about readers in Ireland? Do you recall responses you got from them?

When I wrote *Judith Hearne*—it's never happened since to that extent—I got hundreds of letters from women in America and England and in Ireland saying, "I know somebody like that." A lot of them, I realized, were written by the Judith Hearnes themselves. That response from readers nullified any feeling I had that people were raging at me for having written these books.

When I wrote *The Feast of Lupercal,* censorship of a sort went into effect. Publication was held up for a year because the publishers were afraid the school I had attended might sue me. Some of the masters did want to sue me, and the headmaster said, "This boy's merely biting the hand that birched him." They didn't, of course, sue me. When *The Feast of Lupercal* was published, many boys who had been to the school who were then professionals—

doctors and lawyers, priests—wrote to me or spoke to me saying, "This was a really good book about our school, and we liked it." They were all Catholics, of course, and they were people I wouldn't have thought would have said that. They recognized some sort of truth in the book.

Do you think censorship had any artistic effect on Irish writers, that it ever served as a spur to creativity?

I don't see how it could. If you're not given the right books to read —if I'd never read anything good in modern writing, how could I have been a good modern writer?

For one thing, that repression could have given you something to fight against.

I do think that. I think it was very good for me. I reacted so strongly against the foul system that it gave me a subject.

Then, as I got older, I began to see it differently. Becoming a novelist taught me a sort of objectivity, made me more understanding. But it was good for me to have something to rebel against in my writing.

You said earlier that you believed Ireland needed to look out for moral, religious censorship. Do you think censorship in Ireland was always moral and religious?

It was a sexual censorship; also anything that was considered anticlerical they went out of their way to put down. It created a self-fulfilling hierarchy because boys who went to terrible schools like St. Malachy's became priests. They went on to teach and to treat their pupils as they themselves had been treated and to have the same set of opinions. It's very depressing, I think, particularly since the Irish could be a very funny, happy race, and they're not.

I wonder how many of the things that seem to be wrong with both the Republic and the North now are a result of poor education, a blinkered education, and how many of these prejudices which are frightening exist because of that education. Even though some of my nieces and nephews—they're middle-class people—are inter-marrying with Protestants, I suspect they probably have to tread carefully with each other, husband and wife, because the old preju-dices might rise up—"Catholics are dirty; they have dirty habits." I think in the North of Ireland middle-class people are not religious as they once were. They don't go to church, but the old prejudices are there. The Protestants, of course, are absolutely brainwashed on the idea that Catholics are second-rate people. There's been no real campaign to eradicate that.

The Northern Writer in Exile

You've lived outside Ireland for many years. Did you ever consider living in Northern Ireland or in the Republic?

I've lived in North America and in Europe, in North America mostly, for the last thirty years. I am an expatriate. I left Ulster. There was a choice in Ulster when I was young: you could stay or get out. From the very word go, I wanted to get out. I realized the world was a better place outside of Ulster. I was the first person in my family to emigrate; middle-class people didn't emigrate in those days. I was doing what so many hundreds of thousands of young people are doing today—getting out, going somewhere else. Sure, you lose something. You lose your country in a way, but to my mind, the gains were enormous. I have no regret at not having stayed and lived in Ireland. By going away, I made myself an out-sider. As a writer, to be an outsider, to be an observer, isn't a bad thing. I accepted the fact that I would always be an outsider. I'm not English. When I speak here [in England], the English think hearing my Irish accent that I'm the sort of man who would be deliver-ing their laundry. Nor am I at home in America. The Americans always think I'm British when I speak, so I'm very used to being an outsider.

You never considered living in the South of Ireland, then?

I didn't consider living in the South of Ireland. First of all, because I was anticlerical. And I was terribly bored, as were people of my generation, with all this stuff about the Troubles. It was all over for us—we thought the old Unionist prejudices would be swept aside, and the boring and small-bore nationalism of de Valera and all these Southern Irish people would be swept aside in a new world. We were going to see a world revolution. Communism was going to triumph. All these things were going to happen. De Valera staying out of the war—to people like me brought up in Northern Ireland who had done some reading—seemed a despicable action. I had no sympathy with that at all.

I wrote my first book in Canada, in a cabin in the Laurentians. I was already divorced from Ireland; I had no intention of going back. I was an exile. Once I was in America, I was never going to go back because, for one thing, I could make a living as a writer there much more easily than in Ireland or England. The freedom of America was extraordinary to me at the beginning. I'm not so happy about it now, but it seemed extraordinary then.

Does that mean that you never really thought of the Irish as your audience?

When I was young I gave up on them completely as my audience. I had always felt they wouldn't be my audience because from the very beginning my first book criticized Protestant Ulster. It also criticized Catholic education in Ulster, and my second book did, too. My third book, *The Luck of Ginger Coffey,* criticized the Southern Irish—the impracticality of people who think, because they had some small connections in Ireland, they were going to do very well overseas. So I wasn't surprised that my books were banned, and I didn't really care. There was a feeling in my mind, a feeling that's always been there, that Ireland was a small, repressive country as far as literature was concerned and that to make it in Ireland wasn't enough. There was something wrong with you if you were a "darling" writer. In my childhood I knew that the most popular sort of Irish writers, like Maurice Walsh and Kate O'Brien, were all trashmongers—third rate. I knew that people liked them because they were safe, so I wanted to do something different. I didn't want to be liked in Ireland.

Did the fact that your books were banned affect your sense of literary nationality in any way?

What it did to me was this: in the sixties my wife and I were in Dublin, and I asked her to go into Hanna's—I didn't want to do it myself—and ask them if they had any of my books. They said, "No, he's an American writer, a foreigner." My interest was piqued by this, and we went round to Hodges Figgis. They said, "We think he's a Canadian writer—we're not sure—but we don't have any of his books in now." Here I was, an Irish writer who lived abroad, and my books weren't available in Ireland because nobody thought of me as an Irish writer.

Another embarrassing thing for me was, when I would meet Irish writers abroad, they seemed surprised that I was Irish because my books hadn't been taught in the schools or mentioned in university courses as the work of an Irish writer. They thought I was a Canadian or North American. When I would speak to Irish people and suddenly they'd hear this North of Ireland accent—a strong North of Ireland accent which I've never lost, although I've lived in America for longer than I ever lived in Ireland—I could see the surprise on their faces. When they heard I was called Brian [the Irish pronunciation], not Brian [the English pronunciation], there was also a sort of surprise that I really was a native Indian. That was slightly hurtful.

The fact that Irish writers didn't look upon me as a native son is counterbalanced in my mind by the fact that the English have never treated me as a purely Irish writer. Many Irish writers are taped by the English as regional writers. It's unwitting, just as writers like Stanley Middleton from the north of England are treated as regional writers. I was lucky in that way. Perhaps because the Irish weren't claiming me, because they didn't pay attention to me from the beginning, I was accepted here. I was much more accepted here than I was anywhere else, and I am grateful for that. The Canadians don't think of me as a Canadian writer—"He's not the real thing."

The Americans never accepted me as a North American writer, but, then, the Americans are very parochial in their literary tastes. Ultimately they are only interested in American writers.

If an Irish writer like me is heavily censored at home, he loses his sense of having a literary nationality. Because the Irish didn't accept me as an Irish writer, I didn't think to myself, I'm going to always write about Ireland. I said to myself, I've written my Irish books; I'm living abroad; I must move on.

Would you say, then, that censorship freed you as a writer?

It freed me. I think it freed me and I think it helped me.

You said at one point that when you come back to Ireland now, you return as a tourist.[2] Do you ever feel in any way torn when you come back to Ireland?

No, I don't. I feel an odd thing. When I hear Irish people speak, I feel that, despite everything, I know these people better than I know other peoples. That's all; it's just a feeling. And maybe I don't; maybe I don't. I would like to write another book on Ireland, and maybe I will. I'm very uneasy about it because of the fact that I've been away so long. I suppose the answer to that is, I might make some mistakes in chronology or time, something like that, but I wouldn't make a mistake in my ear for the voice or my knowledge of how people think.

Have you ever taken a public stand against censorship in Ireland or in any other country?

No. I'm very bad in that way. I've never voted anywhere. In Canada I voted for the Social Democratic party; there were only ten of us voting in my ward. I'm not an American citizen, so I can't vote there, and I've never lived in a place except Canada where I had the right to vote. I am by nature hostile to the idea of writers believing that they are public figures and should speak as public figures. I find that "the best lack all conviction, while the worst are full of passionate intensity" [W. B. Yeats]. All these awful people—they're always on committees; they're always on writers' junkets going overseas to speak to other writers.

So you don't see the writer as having a role as an activist.

I don't see myself as having that role. I'm an observer. Being a writer is accepting to live a second-class life. I'm not a doer or a shaker. If I were a doer or a shaker, I wouldn't be a writer. I'd be Mother Teresa. I'd do something. My job, simply, is—I'm a novelist. I chose that a long time ago.

The Principle of Censorship

What is your attitude toward censorship as a matter of principle?

I'm against it of course. Who wouldn't be? I'm against all forms of censorship. I'm totally against it because I think that in sexual matters it encourages a prurience and an unhealthy interest in the subject. Perfect proof is, when hard-core porn came in in the States, it bored the hell out of everyone. I'm against censorship in principle because I think that a civilization should demand as a right that each individual can choose what they want to read or see or do. I think the state should apply censorship only in one case, where the action is truly something we as human beings know to be evil. For instance, snuff movies in the States, where they have people being killed for sexual thrills. Child pornography. Things like that. We all know—we don't have to sit down and have a debate —we know this is not right. I think there's common sense in these matters, and I think the state should use common sense in banning truly perverted pornography. That would be my only caveat.

The minute you introduce common sense you start to get into trouble, though, don't you?

You get into trouble, I know. For instance, I wouldn't stop Jean Marie Le Pen; let him speak to the Tory party. If you stop him speaking, then you could have stopped Nelson Mandela speaking. It's the same thing.

APPENDIX

The Censorship Bill

AE

AE (George Russell) was born in Lurgan, County Armagh, in 1867 and died in England in 1935. A poet and painter, AE was at the centre of the Irish Revival. For many years he worked for the Irish Agricultural Organisation Society, editing two journals that it supported, the *Irish Homestead* and the *Irish Statesman*. AE wrote many of the articles in these journals himself and used them as a forum for discussing not only agriculture but also the state of the nation. When censorship became a political issue in the late 1920s, he opposed it vigorously in editorials such as "The Censorship Bill" in the *Irish Statesman*.

We have never believed that a people could be made moral by Act of Parliament. Real virtue exists only when the soul, having vision both of good and evil, exercising free will, chooses what is good. We believe the man who is constrained to be moral or sober by another is no better in the eyes of Heaven than the man who, in practice, is neither moral nor sober. Whoever lusteth in his heart has already committed the act. The shallow moralists who wish to use force are really materialists who try to defeat divine wisdom. They act as people who do not believe in anything but compulsion. Things which are evil can only truly be combated by creating their opposites. Bad literature may disappear through pure literature being made available. The moralists whose clamour brought about the introduction of the Censorship of Publications Bill no doubt meant well, but what have they done to make noble literature available? In how many counties in Ireland are there public libraries or even book-shops? We are one of the most uncultivated of races, if the

[George Russell], "The Censorship Bill," *Irish Statesman* 10 (1928): 486–87.

quality of our culture can be judged by the number or kind of books read in the Free State. But little could be expected in a country where, until a year or so ago, ninety per cent. of the boys left the national schools at the age of twelve, few of them caring to read or think after. Because there were so few libraries, the majority read little else than newspapers, as books are too heavy reading for the quarter-educated mind. Irish people read the cheapest journals. Instead of providing better reading, our moralists wish to bring about a national censorship, so that cultivated and uncultivated alike will be permitted to read only such books or papers as the State thinks are harmless. If people could be made virtuous by Act of Parliament, we would submit to whatever restrictions might be imposed. But we do not believe evidence can be brought that anywhere censorships over publications have been successful in their objects, and they have always been ridiculous. In practice, the denunciation of a book by the censor increases its publicity. One of the books prohibited in America and Great Britain is James Joyce's "Ulysses." In both countries the book is referred to continually in literary journals. Great numbers of people have read it who, but for the prohibition, would never have heard of it. There are authors and publishers anxious to get their books censored or put in an index for the sake of the advertisement. Every book censored here will become notorious. Its publishers will advertise it as a book prohibited. Our Government may say that they are not concerned with the sale of books in Great Britain or America, but in the Free State. We do not believe censored books can be kept out of the Free State any more than alcohol has been kept out of America by Prohibition. We will have book-leggers where they have boot-leggers. Unless every person who crosses the border or comes in at our ports is examined to his pockets, the books will come in, and just because of their having been censored they will be handed round. That has happened elsewhere. We have no reason to suppose that the State here is capable of greater vigilance than other States with censorships are. What a staff must be retained at the post office or at the ports or at the borders if censored publications are to be kept out! Every parcel must be examined, every pocket searched; and since the importation is made a crime, the person possessing such a book will be deemed to have imported it. Are private houses to be searched for such books if an informer lays an accusation?

A second danger arises because it appears that advertisements, or reviews even, of books dealing with birth control, for example, appearing in a journal will be regarded as reason for the magazine being prohibited. Discussion on this question is common outside Ireland. It is debated at Church of England conferences. Bishops even are divided on it. There are few papers coming into this country which will not have discussion of this question, or reviews of books or advertisement of books, and if the sections of the Bill are strictly adhered to, more than half of the journals coming into Ireland—including papers like *The Times,* the *Daily Telegraph, Manchester Guardian, Observer, Sunday Times,* the *New Statesman,* the *Nation,* or the *Spectator*—would all be liable to suppression because of articles, reports of discussions, reviews or advertisements appearing in them. What a host of enemies will be created. Every journal so suppressed, automatically almost, will become an unfriendly critic of this country and its Government. We have no Irish Press agency established to counteract the effect of anti-Free State propaganda in journals having a much vaster circulation than any Irish papers have abroad. If our own Press was on as high a level morally and intellectually as the papers mentioned, we might not lose much, but such papers are largely read here because a knowledge of world affairs can be acquired from their pages which cannot be acquired here. Any one of these, for all their virtues as newspapers, is liable to suppression for the reasons given above. We ask our readers to think of the effect of such prohibition.

It may be said, "Oh, no, the censorship here will be very wise. It will do nothing foolish." But what does the Bill propose? The State by it is to recognise groups or associations of persons whose business it will be to denounce books or papers to the Minister.[1] What associations are these? Are they associations of intelligent or cultivated men? Or are they associations of fanatics, the associations which have been clamouring for a censorship and seizing and burning excellent journals like the *Observer* and *Sunday Times?* There is possibly not a single member of one of these associations whose opinion on literature would be of any value. Wherever spokesmen of theirs have been reported, they have not talked intelligently. The uniting of their intellectual obscurity into a recognised association will not create a collective wisdom. It merely gives to the group or association an importance that its members individually have not. It merely increases their shouting power, their capacity to disturb the natural wisdom or private judgment of the censors. Then again, the grounds on which books may be denounced are vague. We have some idea of what personal morality is. But we confess we can form no precise idea of what is meant by the sentence which permits a book to be denounced if it "tends to inculcate principles contrary to public morality or is otherwise of such a character that the sale or distribution thereof is or tends to be injurious or detrimental to or subversive of public morality." A sentence like this is very vague. When we are making legal restrictions on the sale of books or magazines there must be precision. There are people who think sincerely that socialistic literature is subversive of public morality. Would a book like Mr. Shaw's *Guide to Socialism* be liable to prohibition? Then again there are people who think sincerely that the literature of agnosticism is subversive of public morality. Are we to have an orthodoxy of thought on such matters? Are the publications of the Rationalist Press liable to suppression because such books run counter to religious belief? We have to be very precise in our definitions. There are thousands of books we read without approving of the ideas. But a disapproval to lead to suppression— that would be revolutionary, and it would itself give birth to other revolutions. Men would conspire against the orthodoxies of opinion the State would impose on them. The interpretation of what is an indecent picture seems to be left to the police. We hope that they will not enter our National Gallery and denounce nudities in plaster, marble or paint. To some people the great defect in the creation of the universe seems to be that we came naked into the world, and not covered with fur. We remember the police denouncing here the engraving of a painting by Sir Frederick Leighton, who was spoken of by Watts as the purest and chastest painter of the nude. The judgment in such matters ought not to be left to the police. There is a mentality here widely spread which considers any attempt to paint a nude figure as indecent. We have seen in Irish houses reproductions of the paintings on the roof of the Sistine Chapel by

Michael Angelo, with breeches and drapery painted over them. The people who did this were more moral than the Popes. We remember the attempts in Dundalk and Cork to prevent the poster of a nude baby reaching for soap being used as an advertisement, and the solemn way in which the bill-posters went to paint breeches on the baby, though in every household in the country the washing of nude babies is a daily occurrence. We do not wish our country to be made ridiculous, and we urge on Deputies and Senators the strictest examination of this Bill and of its consequences both in Ireland and its reactions outside Ireland.

The Censorship
and St. Thomas Aquinas

W. B. Yeats

W. B. Yeats was born in Dublin in 1865 and died in France in 1939. He was awarded the Nobel Prize for literature in 1924. In 1922 Yeats was appointed to the Irish Senate, and in later life he became prominent in public affairs. He was an important voice for civil liberties and human rights, speaking in favour of divorce in 1925 and campaigning against censorship in 1928. In September 1928 he published two articles protesting against censorship in Ireland: one for the English market, "Irish Censorship," which appeared in the *Spectator;* and one for the Irish market, "The Censorship and St. Thomas Aquinas," which appeared in the *Irish Statesman.*

I

"The Censorship of Publications Bill" declares in its preliminary section that "the word 'indecent' shall be construed as including 'calculated to excite sexual passion.'" I know something of the philosophy of St. Thomas, the official philosophy of the Catholic Church. Indeed, the new Thomist movement in literary criticism has made such knowledge almost essential to a man of letters, and I am convinced that this definition, ridiculous to a man of letters, must be sacrilegious to a Thomist. I cannot understand how Catholic lawyers, trained in precision of statement and ecclesiastics, who are supposed to be trained in philosophy, could have committed

W. B. Yeats, "The Censorship and St. Thomas Aquinas," *Irish Statesman* 11 (1928): 47–48. Reprinted in W. B. Yeats, *Uncollected Prose*, vol. 2, *Reviews, Articles and Other Miscellaneous Prose, 1897–1939*, edited by John P. Frayne and Colton Johnson (London: Macmillan, 1975), 477–80. Reprinted by permission of A. P. Watt Ltd. on behalf of Michael B. Yeats and Macmillan London Ltd. and by permission of the editors.

such a blunder. Had Professor Trench made it I would understand, for his sort of evangelical belief, whatever it owes to the ascetic Platonism of the seventeenth century, owes nothing to Aquinas.[1]

II

Cardinal Mercier writes in his *Manual of Modern Scholastic Philosophy,* Vol. 1, p. 314, English Edition: "Plato and Descartes, who both considered the soul as a substance completely distinct from the body, make it reside in some central part whence, like a pilot at the helm, it can control the movements of the whole organism. By Plato the rational soul is placed in the brain, whilst Descartes relegates it to the minute portion of it called the pineal gland. St. Thomas's opinion, to which we adhere, is entirely different; he lays down that the soul is wholly present in the whole body and in all its parts—'anima rationalis est tota in toto corpore et tota in qualibet parte corporis.'"

For centuries the Platonizing theology of Byzantium had dominated the thought of Europe. Amidst the abstract splendour of its basilicas stood saints with thought-tortured faces and bodies that were but a framework to sustain the patterns and colours of their clothes. The mosaics of the Apse displayed a Christ with face of pitiless intellect, or a pinched, flat-breasted virgin holding a child like a wooden doll. Nobody can stray into that little Byzantium chapel at Palermo, which suggested the chapel of the Grail to Wagner, without for an instant renouncing the body and all its works and sending all thought up into that heaven the pseudo Dionysius, the Areopagite, fashioned out of the Platonic ideas.

III

Within fifty years of the death of St. Thomas the art of a vision had faded, and an art of the body, an especial glory of the Catholic Church, had inspired Giotto. The next three centuries changed the likeness of the Virgin from that of a sour ascetic to that of a woman so natural nobody complained when Andrea del Sarto chose for his model his wife, or Raphael his mistress, and represented her with all the patience of his "sexual passion." A corresponding change in technique enabled him to imagine her, not as if drawn upon a flat surface, but as though moulded under the hand in bas-relief. Painters liberated from a conviction that only ideas were real, painted, from the time of Orcagna, bodies that seemed more and more tangible till at last Titian saw grow upon his canvas an entirely voluptuous body. "Anima est in *toto* corpore" (the italics are Cardinal Mercier's). "The breast's superb abundance where a man might base his head." The lawyers who drew up the Bill, and any member of the Dáil or Senate who thinks of voting for it, should study in some illustrated history of Art Titian's *Sacred and Profane Love,* and ask themselves if there is no one it could not incite to "sexual passion," and if they answer, as they are bound to, that there are many ask this further question of themselves. Are we prepared to exclude such art from Ireland and to sail in a ship of fools, fools that dressed bodies Michael Angelo left naked, Town Councillors of Montreal who hid the Discobulus in the cellar?

IV

There is such a thing as immoral painting and immoral literature, and a criticism growing always more profound establishes that they are bad paintings and bad literature, but though it may be said of them that they sin always in some way against "in *toto* corpore," they cannot be defined in a sentence. If you think it necessary to exclude certain books and pictures, leave it to men learned in art and letters, if they will serve you, and, if they will not, to average educated men. Choose what men you may, they will make blunders, but you need not compel them to with a definition.

The Censorship

George Bernard Shaw

George Bernard Shaw was born in Dublin in 1856 and died in England in 1950. He received the Nobel Prize for literature in 1926. Several of Shaw's plays were banned in England by the Lord Chamberlain, including *Mrs. Warren's Profession* and *The Shewing-up of Blanco Posnet*. The latter was staged successfully in 1909 at the Abbey Theatre in defiance of the ban. In 1933 Shaw's novel *The Adventures of the Black Girl in Her Search for God* was banned in Ireland. Throughout his life Shaw was a vehement opponent of censorship in both Britain and Ireland. He wrote at length on British censorship in his preface to *The Shewing-up of Blanco Posnet*.

It is a convention to assume that there is nothing people like more than political liberty. As a matter of fact there is nothing they dread more. Under the feeble and apologetic tyranny of Dublin Castle we Irish were forced to endure a considerable degree of compulsory freedom.[1] The moment we got rid of that tyranny we rushed to enslave ourselves. We gave our police power to seize any man's property and to put upon him the onus of proving that it belonged to him. We declared that as prison would not deter Irishmen from evildoing they must be savagely flogged; and when evildoers were flogged they were imprisoned for long periods lest the flogging should provoke them to commit fresh crimes. When gunmen were all over the place we made it a crime for anyone to possess a weapon to protect himself against gunmen. We are too much afraid of our peaceful citizens to arm them, and too much afraid of brawlers not to suspect a brawler in every peaceful citizen. We are afraid to let a fellow citizen practise fine art because he (or she) might

G. Bernard Shaw, "The Censorship," *Irish Statesman* 11 (1928): 206–8. Reprinted by permission of The Society of Authors on behalf of the Bernard Shaw Estate.

take advantage of our ignorance of art to cheat or corrupt us. Miss Mia Cranwill, the Irish Benvenuto Cellini (I am not referring to her private life) is to be driven out of the country by the sellers of the dullest and commonest English silver goods under a regulation which a medieval guild in the last stage of decay would have refused to believe possible in a sane community.

We shall never be easy until every Irish person is permanently manacled and fettered, gagged and curfewed, lest he should punch our heads or let out the truth about something. It is useless to remonstrate. As Mark Twain said, the average man is a coward. The latest demonstration of Irish abjectness is the supplanting of constitutional law by the establishment of a Censorship extending in general terms to all human actions, but specifically aimed at any attempt to cultivate the vital passion of the Irish people or to instruct it in any function which is concerned with that passion. It is, in short, aimed at the extermination of the Irish people as such to save them from their terror of life and of one another. The Jews aspired to a state in which "none should make them afraid"; but they proposed to live to enjoy it, each Jew sitting up, alive and hearty, under his own vine and fig tree. We hope for no peace until we lie dead, each under his own headstone, forgetting that when it comes to the point we shall be afraid to die lest the devil should use us worse than even our dreaded fellow-creatures.

Since it would be vain to appeal to the Irish people, I turn to the Church, which is not Irish, but Catholic. Is it going to submit to this amateur Inquisition which is eliciting triumphant chuckles of "We told you so" from Ulster? Does it realize the ghastly change that threatens its temples in the Unfree State at the suggestion of Sir William Joynson Hicks, the most resolute No Popery man in England, and of a raving Orangeman who supplies Ireland with English papers and declares that he would rather murder his children than trust them uncensored.[2] I am on cordial personal terms with both of these sturdy Protestants; but I hardly expected to see the Catholic Church coming to heel at their whistle.

All those figures of the dead Christ, with their strong appeal to the pity and love of Irish girls (who has not seen them weeping and praying before such figures?) must be melted or smashed, and the girls referred to St. Thomas Aquinas for instruction in purely intellectual religious emotion. All the handsome brave St. Joans must be chopped up for firewood. The boys who feel that they can pray to St. Joan when they cannot pray with any heart to the distantly august Trinity will cease to pray, and interest themselves in getting rich quickly. The Catherines and Margarets with their long tresses, teaching the young to associate loveliness with blessedness, will be torn down, leaving their adorers to associate loveliness with debauchery, like all Censors. The Mother of God herself will be spared only on condition that she be made repulsively ugly lest she should "excite sexual passion," a course which must end in her complete banishment lest the ugliness should excite abhorrence. The Faith will wither at the root and perish. The Iconoclast will rejoice and exult.

Then what of the priest? Clearly his splendid vestments at the altar cannot be tolerated by the Censors: his carnal good looks must be masked in Genevan black. The gilded shrine must be replaced by a cricket pavilion locker and the incense replaced by assafoetida; for did not Mahomet say "There are three supremely delightful things: perfume, woman, and prayer; and the greatest of these delights is prayer." And what is incense but perfume? Clearly if Mahomet had been an Irishman he would not have wasted his time praying when he could get all his soul's troubles settled for him by a Censorship.

As to singing in churches, its sensuous appeal must be severely censored under the Act. In London the contrast between the virility and charm of the singing in Westminster Cathedral and the wretched bawling of the opera choruses has struck everyone who has compared them; and I cannot believe that the Irish cathedrals do not equally eclipse the Gaiety Theatre. But under the Censorship the Mass will be sung in Ireland by the choristers of the musical comedy stage, because their efforts could not possibly warm the most susceptible female heart.

These fleshly and artistic snares of the devil are, however, mere trifles? What of the priest as confessor, counsellor, spiritual adviser, teacher of youth? If innocent youths or maidens going from a sheltered home into the world are warned by their pastor of the perils of venereal disease, away with him to prison for corrupting the young. If the wives and husbands of his congregation come to him for help in the domestic troubles brought on them by their ignorance, and he brings the ancient wisdom of his Church to their relief (his supply of modern scientific treatises on the subject being cut off) away with him at once: the priest who would mention such things in conversation with a lady is no better than Dr. Marie Stopes. If, in his counsels to schoolboys, he makes any reference to homosexuality, unfrock him and cast him forth to share an eternity of burning brimstone with Miss Radclyffe Hall.

And when all these monstrous follies are being perpetrated by way of purifying Ireland the Church will be blamed for it. Already it is said on all hands that the Censorship Bill is the Church's doing. It will certainly be the Church's undoing unless the Church stands openly by its anti-Puritan tradition. The notion that Raphael was less inspired, or otherwise inspired, when he painted the history of Cupid and Psyche than when he painted the Transfiguration, has no warrant in Church doctrine.

(By the way, what is to be done with the National Gallery under the Act?)

What we have to consider in judging the special aim of the Bill is that life, especially married life, is unnecessarily troubled and occasionally wrecked because we have no technique of marriage; and this ignorance is produced by the deliberate suppression of all responsible information on the subject. England has an expert instructress in the person of Dr. Marie Stopes; and the result is that —quite apart from the special technique of Birth Control, which she has at all events rescued from the uncontradicted, and in Ireland presently to become the legally uncontradictable, advertisements of the underground trade in "specialities"—numbers of unhappy marriages have been set right by her instruction. The Irish people will not be allowed to consult either Dr. Stopes or their spiritual directors. Of clandestine instruction there will be plenty; but as nobody will be allowed to criticise it, or even to mention it, everything that is evil in it will be protected and nourished, and everything that is honest and enlightening in it will be discredited and suppressed.

But we must not let our vision be narrowed by the specific and avowed objects of the Act, which are, to prevent our learning the truth about the various methods of Birth Control (some of them in urgent need of criticism) now in irresistible use, and to hide from us the natural penalties of prostitution until we have irrevocably incurred them, often quite innocently at second hand. The matter of Censorship as opposed to constitutional law is bigger than these, its meanest instances. Ireland is now in a position of special and extreme peril. Until the other day we enjoyed a factitious prestige as a thorn in the side of England, or shall I say, from the military point of view, the Achilles heel of England? We were idealized by Pity, which always idealizes the victim and the underdog. The island was hymned as one of saints, heroes, bards, and the like more or less imaginary persons. Every Don Quixote in Europe and America, and even actually in China, made a Dulcinea of Kathleen ni Houlihan and the Dark Rosaleen. We thought ourselves far too clever to take ourselves at the Quixotic valuation; but in truth even the most cynically derisive Dubliners (detestable animals!) overrated us very dangerously; and when we were given a free hand to make good we found ourselves out with a shock that has taken all the moral pluck out of us as completely as physical shell shock. We can recover our nerve only by forcing ourselves to face new ideas, proving all things, and standing by that which is good. We are in a world in which mechanical control over nature and its organization has advanced more in a single century than it had done before in a whole epoch. But the devil of it is that we have made no corresponding advance in morals and religion. We are abject cowards when confronted with new moral ideas, and insanely brave when we go out to kill one another with a physical equipment of artificial volcanoes and atmospheres of poison, and a mental equipment appropriate to stone axes and flint arrow heads. We incite our young men to take physical risks which would have appalled the most foolhardy adventurers of the past; but when it is proposed to allow a young woman to read a book which treats sexual abnormalities as misfortunes to be pitied instead of horrors to be screamed at and stoned, an Irishman arises in the face of England and madly declares that he is prepared in the interests of family life to slay his children rather than see them free to read such a work. What sort of family life his daughter has led him since he made this amazing exhibition of Irish moral panic is a matter for shuddering conjecture; but however dearly he has paid at his own fireside for his terrors, he can hardly have got worse than he deserves.

The moral is obvious. In the nineteenth century all the world was concerned about Ireland. In the twentieth, nobody outside Ireland cares twopence what happens to her. If she holds her own in the front of European culture, so much the better for her and for Europe. But if, having broken England's grip of her, she slops back into the Atlantic as a little grass patch in which a few million moral cowards are not allowed to call their souls their own by a handful of morbid Catholics, mad with heresyphobia, unnaturally combining with a handful of Calvinists mad with sexphobia (both being in a small and intensely disliked minority of their own co-religionists) then the world will let "these Irish" go their own way into insignificance without the smallest concern. It will no longer even tell funny stories about them. That was what happened to so mighty a power as the Spanish Empire: and in magnitude we are to the Spanish Empire what a crumb is to a loaf.

By the way, the reality behind that poetic fiction, "the Irish race," has a good deal of Spanish blood in it. The seed of Torquemada is in the Irish soil as well as the seed of Calvin.

Let us beware!

The Irish Censorship

Liam O'Flaherty

Liam O'Flaherty was born on the Aran Islands in 1896 and died in Dublin in 1984. In the 1920s O'Flaherty became attracted to communism, and in 1930 he became the first Irish novelist to have his work censored in Ireland. Much of his fiction was banned throughout the thirties and forties, including *The House of Gold* (1929), *The Puritan* (1931), and *Land* (1946). O'Flaherty, who was best known as a short story writer, throughout his career wrote in both Irish and English. He published little new work after the 1950s.

During the Eucharistic Congress recently held in Dublin, I was staying in a small Kerry town.[1] It has a population of two thousand people and fifty-three public houses. Like almost every other Irish provincial town, it is incredibly dirty and sordid to look upon. In the long back street inhabited by the proletariat I came across human excrement at every second step. There was no vestige of culture in the place. The three local priests were sour and secretive fellows, who confined their activities to the prevention of fornication, dancing and reading. The only pastime permitted to the males was drinking in the fifty-three public houses. The females wandered about with a hungry expression in their eyes. Shortly after my arrival, the priests of the diocese held a mass dinner at my hotel, to devise ways and means for getting me out of the county, as a menace to faith and morals; but without any success.

Then the Eucharistic Congress came along and the populace, exalted by some extraordinary fanaticism, decorated the town with bunting. In the proletarian slum, several altars were erected in the

Liam O'Flaherty, "The Irish Censorship," *The American Spectator* 1 (November 1932): 2. Reprinted by permission of the Peters Fraser & Dunlop Group Ltd.

open air. Around these altars some people recited the rosary at night, while others played accordions, danced and drank stout.

However, no attempt was made to remove the dung from the streets, nor any fraction of the dirt which desecrated the walls of the houses and the floors of the taverns. I walked up and down the town, pointing from the bunting to the pavement and saying: "Bunting, dung. Dung, bunting." It was considered sacrilegious.

Unclean offal of any sort, whether in my neighborhood or in the minds of people with whom I have association, is strongly distasteful to me. So is poverty, ungracious tyranny and ignoble suffering. In my work I have been forced in honesty to hold up a mirror to life as I found it in my country. And, of necessity, the mirror shows the dung about the pretty altars. So a censorship has been imposed upon my work, since it is considered sacrilegious by the Irish Church that I should object to the sordid filth around the altars.

The tyranny of the Irish Church and its associate parasites, the upstart Irish bourgeoisie, the last posthumous child from the wrinkled womb of European capitalism, maintains itself by the culture of dung, superstition and ignoble poverty among the masses. And the censorship of literature was imposed, lest men like me could teach the Irish masses that contact with dung is demoralizing, that ignorance is ignoble and that poverty, instead of being a passport to Heaven, makes this pretty earth a monotonous Hell. The soutaned bullies of the Lord, fortressed in their dung-encrusted towns, hurl the accusation of sexual indecency at any book that might plant the desire for civilization and freedom in the breasts of their wretched victims.

So they have set up a censorship of books in Ireland, and now at Irish ports, whose sole export is porter and men of genius, imported literature which is the product of Irish genius is seized and burned as dangerous contraband. And so tortured Ireland, which a few years ago asked for and received the sympathy of the world's intellectuals, now shows herself as a surly, sick bitch biting the hand that fed her.

But it's not true of Ireland, nor of the mass of Irishmen and Irishwomen. Slaves cannot be blamed for the vices of their masters. I am censored and abhorred by the illiterate ruffians who control Irish life at present. There is hardly a single newspaper in Ireland that would dare print anything I write. There is hardly a bookshop in Ireland that would dare show my books in its windows. There is hardly a library that would not be suppressed for having my books on its shelves. Outside Dublin not a single organization would dare ask me to address them. Yet I claim that Ireland is the only country where I feel of any consequence as a writer. It is the only country where I feel the youth and freshness of Spring among the people, where I feel at one with my mates, where I sing with their singing and weep with their weeping, where I feel that I am a good workman doing a useful job and honored for my craft.

Ireland is no land of barbarians and there are no people in the world who love art and beauty more than the Irish. But alas! Our little island has been stricken with a triple mange of friars, gombeen men and poverty. The soutaned witch-doctors have spread terror among our simple folk and, as one goes through the country, it is pathetic to meet in every little town and village timid, whispering individuals who say, "It's terrible here. I can't get anything to read on account of the priests. Have you got any of your books you could lend me?" In the same way, I was told by an eminent London publisher that he receives bundles of letters from sexually-starved Irishwomen, asking for bawdy books. Booklegging may soon become on a small scale quite as profitable as the prohibition of alcohol made bootlegging in America.

Bawdy books! Bawdy houses! Booze! On these three forms of vulgar entertainment there seemed to be no censorship whatsoever during the Eucharistic Congress in Dublin. The town was wide open all night and every night. Then the mob went back home to purify themselves by scratching their backs against hair shirts. The militant puritans in Ireland have, in my opinion, staged their last great parade. Before very long they'll be all hurled into the clean Atlantic, together with their censorship, their dung, their bawdy books, their bawdy houses and their black booze. Then we can once more in Ireland have wine and love and poetry; become a people famed, as of old, "for beauty and amorousness."

Censorship
in the Saorstat

Samuel Beckett

Samuel Beckett was born in Foxrock, County Dublin, in 1906 and died in Paris in 1989. He received the Nobel Prize for literature in 1969. Three of his works were banned in Ireland: *More Pricks Than Kicks* (1934), *Watt* (1953), and *Molloy* (1954). In 1935 he was commissioned by the *Bookman* to write "Censorship in the Saorstat" (the Saorstat was the Irish name given to the Irish Free State from 1922 to 1948). The *Bookman* went out of business, however, and the article was not published until 1983. Beckett's more recent work includes *Stirrings Still* (1989).

An act to make provision for the prohibition of the sale and distribution of unwholesome literature and for that purpose to provide for the establishment of a censorship of books and periodical publications, and to restrict the publication of reports of certain classes of judicial proceedings and for other purposes incidental to the aforesaid. (16th July, 1929)[1]

The Act has four parts.

Part 1 emits the definitions, as the cuttle squirts ooze from its cod. E.g., "the word 'indecent' shall be construed as including suggestive of, or inciting to sexual immorality or unnatural vice or likely in any other similar way to corrupt or deprave." Deputies and Senators can seldom have been so excited as by the problem of how to make the definitive form of this litany orduretight. Tate and Brady would not slip through it now if the Minister for Justice deemed they ought not. A plea for distinction between inde-

Samuel Beckett, "Censorship in the Saorstat" in *Disjecta: Miscellaneous Writings and a Dramatic Fragment by Samuel Beckett,* edited by Ruby Cohn (London: John Calder, 1983), 84–88. Reprinted by permission of John Calder (Publishers) Ltd. and Grove Weidenfeld.

cency obiter and ex professo did not detain a caucus that has bigger and better things to split than hairs, the pubic not excepted. "It is the author's expressed purpose, it is the effect which his thought will have as expressed in the particular words into which he has *flung* (eyetalics mine) his thought that the censor has to consider." (Minister for Justice)

Part 2 deals with the constitution of and procedure to be adopted by the Censorship of Publications Board, the genesis of prohibition orders, the preparation of a register of prohibited publications and the issuing of search warrants in respect of prohibited publications.

The Board shall consist of five fit and proper persons. This figure was arrived at only after the most animated discussion. Twelve was proposed as likely to form a more representative body. But the representative principle was rejected, notably by Deputy Professor Tierney, who could not bear the thought of any committee with only half a Jew upon it. This is a great pity, as the jury convention would have ensured the sale of at least a dozen copies in this country, assuming, as in reverence bound, that the censors would have gone to bed simultaneously and independently with the text, and not passed a single copy of the work from hand to hand, nor engaged a fit and proper person to read it to them in assembly. "Fit and proper" would seem to denote nothing less than highly qualified in common sense, "specialists in common sense" (Dep. Prof. Alton). Dep. J. J. Byrne burst all his buttons in this connexion: "Give me the man broad-minded and fair who can look at the thing from a common sense point of view. If you want to come to a proper conclusion upon what is for the good of the people in a question of this kind, I unhesitatingly *plump* for the common sense man." This is getting dangerously close to the opinion of Miss Robey, that for the artist as for the restaurateur the customer is always right. Imagine if you are able, and being able care to, Dep. J. J. Byrne's selection coming to the proper conclusion with reference say to the *Secret Life* of Procopius, a work that has so far evaded the net. His position would be as invidious as that of Jerome reading Cicero, for which he was whipped by the devil in a Lenten dream, were it not that the man broad-minded and fair is at liberty to withdraw his purities from the pollution before they are entirely spent, that is to say almost at once. "It is not necessary for any sensible individual to read the whole of a book before coming to the conclusion whether the book is good, bad or indifferent." (Dep. J. J. Byrne) "There are books which are so blatantly indecent and known to be indecent that it would be unnecessary for the members of the Board to read every line of them. Should the members of the Board, for instance, be compelled to read through every line of *Ulysses,* a book that has been universally condemned?" (Minister for Justice). The judicial outlook. Dep. J. J. Byrne's censor's Lenten dream will not wake him.

The stock allusion to the *Decameron* caused no little flutter in the Senate, but was skilfully negotiated by Senator Johnson: "I do not think it has any great reputation as a book, and so with re-gard to many other books," and by the Minister for Justice: "some of Boccaccio's stories, I understand, are quite excellent, e.g., the plaintive tale of Patient Griselda."

The Bill as originally drafted provided for complaints to be made with reference to obscene publications via recognized associations, something in the style of the Irish Commercial Travellers' Federa-tion, a kind of St. Vincent de Paul de Kock Societies. In so far as this clause was spewed out of the Dail and actually not reinserted p.r. by the Senate, any individual is now in theory entitled to lodge a complaint on his own bottom. But as this would entail his procuring five copies of the work for submission to the Board, he finds him-self obliged, precisely as the original Bill intended, to cast around for some body whose interest in the public state of mind condones, more amply than his own, a small outlay. And behold the Catholic Truth Society, transformed into an angel of light, stands at his right hand. Precisely as the original Bill intended.

The Register of Prohibited Publications is a most happy idea, constituting as it does, after the manner of Boston's Black Book, a free and permanent advertisement of those books and periodicals in which, be their strictly literary status never so humble, inheres the a priori excellence that they have annoyed the specialist in common sense. I may add that it is the duty of every customs official in the Saorstat to exhibit on demand this Register to the incoming mug.

Part 3 sets forth with loving care the restrictions on publication of reports of judicial proceedings. No longer may the public lap up the pathological titbit or the less frigid proceedings for divorce, nullity of marriage, judicial separation and restitution of conjugal rights. No sports less indoor than these engross, even in our evening papers, such space as survives the agitation of protective tariffs, subsidies, monopolies and quotas and the latest snuffles from the infant industries at Drogheda, Navan, Dundalk, Mullingar, Westport, Edenderry, Slane, Ennis, Athy, Newbridge, Nenagh, Portarlington, Tuam, Mallow, Thurles (two syllables), Arklow, Aughrim, Portlaw, Killaloe, Enniscorthy, Carrickmacross, Carrick-on-Suir, Ballyboghill and Bray, e.o.o.e.

Part 4 enshrines the essence of the Bill and its exciting cause, in the general heading tactfully enveloped among the "other purposes incidental," the prohibition namely of publications advocating the use of contraceptives, blushing away beyond the endurance of the most dogged reader among the Miscellaneous and General. France may commit race suicide, Erin will never. And should she be found at any time deficient in Cuchulains, at least it shall never be said that they were contraceived. Thus to waive the off chance of a reasonable creature is no longer a mere mortal sin, but a slapup social malfeasance, with corollary in the civic obligation to throttle reason itself whenever it happens to be "flung" into a form obnoxious to the cephalopods of state. The pure Gael, drawing his breath from his heels, will never be permitted to defile his mind with even such fairly clean dirt as the *Black Girl in her Search for God* so long as he can glorify his body to the tune of half a dozen byblows, white as pthisis, in search for a living. This yoke will not irk him.

Such is the cream of a measure that the Grand Academy of Balnibarbi could hardly have improved on. Even if it worked, which needless to say it does not, it would do so gratis, an *actum agere* regardless of expense. For the Irish are a characteristic agricultural community in this, that they have something better to do than read and that they produce a finished type of natural fraudeur having nothing to learn from the nice discriminations of Margaret Sanger and Marie Carmichael Stopes, D. Sc., Ph. D., F. R. S. Litt., etc.[2] Doubtless there is something agreeable to the eye in this failure to function to no purpose, the broken handpump in the free air station. Paley's watch in the desert is charming, but the desert in Paley's watch still more so. Whether a government of the people by the people can afford these free shows is another matter.

Finally to amateurs of morbid sociology this measure may appeal as a curiosity of panic legislation, the painful tension between life and thought finding issue in a constitutional belch, the much reading that is a weariness exorcised in 21 sections. Sterilization of the mind and apotheosis of the litter suit well together. Paradise peopled with virgins and the earth with decorticated multiparas.

The Register as on the 30th September 1935 shows 618 books and 11 periodicals under the ban. Among men, women and for all I know children of letters writing in English, the most liberally advertised are: Aldous Huxley, the Powys brothers, Maugham, John Dos Passos, Aldington, Sinclair Lewis, Wyndham Lewis, William Faulkner, D. H. Lawrence, Wells, Chaucer (Eve), Kay Boyle, Middleton Murry and Mae West. Irish authors deemed from time to time unwholesome are: O'Flaherty, O'Casey, O'Leary, O Faolain (no apostrophe), Shaw, Clarke and Moore (George). Foreign writers distinguished in all English versions are: Döblin, both Zweigs, Gaston Leroux, Gorki, Leonhard Frank, Roth, Rolland, Romains, Barbusse, Schnitzler, Hamsun, Colette, Casanova, Céline, all contributors to the Spanish Omnibus, Jarry, Boccaccio, Dékobra and the incomparable Vicki. With regard to scientific works it need only be said that all the most up to date enchiridions both of marriage and of love are here, from Bertrand Russell's to Ralph de Pomerai's. Of the banned periodicals perhaps the most keenly missed have been, pending the expiration (if any) of the Prohibition Order: *Ballyhoo, Health and Efficiency, Broadway and Hollywood Movies, Health and Strength, Empire News, incorporating the Umpire, Thompson's Weekly,* and *True Romances.*

My own registered number is 465, number four hundred and sixty-five, if I may presume to say so.

We now feed our pigs on sugarbeet pulp. It is all the same to them.

The Mart of Ideas

Sean O'Faolain

Sean O'Faolain was born in Cork in 1900 and now lives in Dublin. Several of his works of fiction were banned in Ireland, including *Midsummer Night Madness* (1932) and *Bird Alone* (1936). From the 1940s to the 1960s, he was the most important voice against censorship in Ireland. In the *Bell,* the magazine he edited from 1940 to 1946, he repeatedly condemned Irish censorship in editorials such as "The Mart of Ideas." His later works include *I Remember! I Remember!* (1961), *Vive Moi!* (1964), and *Foreign Affairs and Other Stories* (1976).

It is one of the most dangerous illusions of your man of action that he can starve the public mind and keep its conscience alive. He will hope to rely on the public to boycott a Black Market in goods while he himself runs a Black Market in ideas. For that is how the illusion works in any country where only the few, usually economically independent, are given free access to ideas and where intellectual indifference is encouraged as a virtue in the masses. One clear sign that this intellectual indifferentism to ideas is being encouraged is the contempt of the public for anything which is not a popular political issue, and it was illustrated here a little while ago when somebody declared that the average man in this country does not care a rap about the Literary Censorship. If he was correct he should have wrung his hands with sorrow. Instead he was, apparently, quite pleased.

This attitude to ideas is based, ultimately, on the theory that the public can be divided into those who do not think, those who do not care, and those who act. At the top are the intelligentsia. These,

[Sean O'Faolain] "The Mart of Ideas," *Bell* 4 (June 1942): 153–57. Reprinted by permission of A. P. Watt Ltd. and by Curtis Brown Ltd. on behalf of Sean O'Faolain. © 1942 by Sean O'Faolain.

since they *do* think are dangerous people, and therefore they are commonly mocked. "Our pseudo-intellectuals"; "the intelligentsia, God-help-us"; "the literary cliques"; "our scribbling journalists." How well one knows the contemptuous phrases, all intended to suggest that they do not, in fact, think at all—are, in brief, charlatans. At the bottom are the masses who can be kept quiet with bread and circuses. In between are the men of action who do the real work of the country. Now, nobody will deny that in most countries the mass of the people are, in normal times, indifferent to almost every plea that does not concern their own comfort. But it is astonishing that anybody should think this indifference a matter of no importance. Indeed, time and again, even your man of action comes up against it, as when in an hour of crisis, forgetting how long he has played upon that indifference, even counted on it in the tactics of his benevolent despotism, he will suddenly begin to assault his public with the most honourable and intelligent arguments. And nobody is more pained than he is if his pleadings fall on deaf ears. Look out of any office-window. Those crowds who pass and re-pass—it is of those that any man may say that not one in a thousand cares tuppence about such things as the Literary Censorship. But if there are also thousands who do not care tuppence about the Black Market, the Gaelic Language, A.R.P. [Air Raid Precautions], the Licensing Laws—except in so far as it is fun to break them— is it not simply because they never do consider? And how can you possibly expect any man to think about the Black Market when for thirteen years you have been employing a Literary Censorship to keep him from thinking about anything at all?

There is no connection between the two? Ah, but there is. There is this danger of encouraging people "not to care." For it is not a question of whether what they do not care about is, or is not, in itself, of vital importance. Three weeks ago, for example, Eugene O'Neill's "Mourning Becomes Electra" was staged in one of our provincial cities. In two churches condemnatory sermons were preached about the play, presumably because it dealt with an incest theme. I am quite certain that these good provincial audiences have no more than a very mild academic interest in incest, and that the greater part of them hardly knew, or even still know, what it is. Ignorance of the subject would therefore be small loss to them.

But, what an attitude, to want to cherish their ignorance! What it amounts to is "Don't think about anything that does not concern you." Combined with the implication that there is very little which does concern us. And although it is, indeed, very pleasant and easy to have such an obedient and innocent populace, surely if their obedience and innocence is automatic, i.e., based on indifference and not on an intelligent appreciation of what is involved, it will inevitably crack when they do come face to face with some difficult task which *does* concern them. And then it becomes futile, because it is too late, for your man of action to argue and plead on reasonable grounds, since he has for years been deliberately nourishing what is tantamount to a contradiction in terms—a brainless morale, a moronic mass to which he can make no intelligent appeal whatever.

If the reader hesitates to believe that this kind of populace is being created I would ask him how long it is since he has himself heard, or heard of, a frank, *public* discussion of any three of the following subjects—Birth Control, Freemasonry, The Knights of Columbanus, Unmarried Mothers, Illegitimacy, Divorce, Homosexuality, Rhythm, Lunacy, Libel, Euthanasia, Prostitution, Venereal Disease, or even Usury—to take only a few subjects which do concern us closely. Surely it is the fact that we are not having enough public discussion of all sorts of things that breeds the "not caring" attitude? Surely it is this indifferentism that made it possible for a pamphlet issued recently by one of the best-known organisations in the country, the Gaelic League, to say—with the amiable idiocy of a mental sleep-walker—"But is there such a thing as Europe? It seems all very remote now except in terms of newspaper reports and air-raids?"

Thirty years ago nobody would have denied the importance of a live intelligentsia here. Then those same people who now deride it made use of it day in and day out to disseminate all those doctrines which have resulted in a free Eire. That intelligentsia exists still; small; naturally uneven as it always is; composed of every man and woman who keeps his brains burnished and is neither so snobbish, nor so cautious, as to hide his light under a bushel; every paper and every periodical in the country is a member of it—though what each sells is of course a very difficult matter, and the investor has to be supremely cautious lest he should suddenly wake up to find that he has been dealing for years with a Bucket Shop. For in this mart there is no Committee to elect members, and every man who opens his mouth in public is a legitimate broker.

And that, of course, indicates the whole point and purpose of the Literary Censorship as it is worked. It does not propose to defend fair-trading in ideas. It does not aim at making ideas more easily marketable. It does not aim at establishing a smooth machinery for their interchange but rather, a smooth machinery to prevent their interchange. And, of course, it could, even under the present Act, and would if the public demanded it, do these positive things. It could, for example, assist publishers by allowing them to present manuscripts for pre-publication inspection. It could, and is, in chosen cases, actually supposed to open up negotiation with authors and publishers. It never does. It could take into account the aims and intentions of writers, and again is supposed to do so, but does not. It may revise its decisions—but never once, in the case of a book, has it done this. All of which omissions have turned it into a wholly negative and destructive piece of machinery; and all of which it has done and failed to do because people "do not care."

We beg anybody who may be glad at this "not caring" to revise his ideas. After all, if a man is not interested in the Literary Censorship, why should he be interested in any public issue at all?

It is not too sweeping to say that ideas, as we will agree if we have anything of sane idealism in us, are the substance of life. They do not come from the bottom upwards. They come from quiet corners of life which make no fuss, and seep slowly downward to inform the whole of society. To give a tiny example, when Ann says to Angel "I have a complex about such-and-such," it does not occur to either of them that they are, for the moment, dominated by the minds of two or three old professors in Western Europe. It is against all such, against every man who takes life seriously, who takes thought seriously, who takes art and culture seriously, that the Literary Censorship is directed by those who would establish in place of thought a rigid orthodoxy that no man must even discuss, let alone question or deny. For any man to say, to be pleased, that nobody cares about that is, in the absolutely literal sense, to take leave of his senses. It is to prepare the way for the handing over of all power to the caucus and the mob.

Frank O'Connor
on Censorship

Frank O'Connor

Frank O'Connor (Michael O'Donovan) was born in Cork in 1903 and died in Dublin in 1966. From the 1940s to the 1960s many of his works were banned in Ireland, including *Dutch Interior* (1940), *The Midnight Court* (1946), *The Common Chord* (1947), *Traveller's Samples* (1951), and *Kings, Lords and Commons* (1961). The banning of *The Midnight Court* and of *Kings, Lords and Commons* created widespread controversy because the translation of a classic Gaelic text was being censored; in addition, O'Connor was at the centre of the 1942 censorship debate over the publication of *The Tailor and Ansty.*

On Wednesday, February 14th, 1962, in Trinity College, Dublin, at a meeting of the College Historical Society, Mr. Frank O'Connor proposed the motion "that Irish censorship is insulting to Irish intelligence." The motion was opposed by the Hon. Mr. Justice Kevin Haugh.[1] It was carried by forty votes to nine. We publish here the text of Mr. O'Connor's speech:

My Lord, Gentlemen of the Jury—

One day during my time as a librarian a young man asked to see me. He wanted to complain of an indecent book. I asked him what was indecent about it, and he said there was a dirty word in it. I asked where and he replied promptly "Page 164." Obviously page 164 had imprinted itself indelibly on his brain. I read the page and asked "Which word?" He said "That word" and he pointed to the word "navel." I felt sorry for him and wanted to ask him whether

Frank O'Connor, "Frank O'Connor on Censorship," *The Dubliner* (March 1962): 39–44. Reprinted by permission of the Peters Fraser & Dunlop Group Ltd.

he couldn't find some nice girl to walk out with, but I decided it might be dangerous. I didn't feel he had reached the age for girls. Perhaps what he needed was a dolly with changeable diapers to practise on.

Unfortunately, as any public librarian will tell you, that young man wasn't exceptional any more than the critic of the *Freeman's Journal* who reviewed *The Playboy of the Western World* and said that the word "shift" was one that no modest Irishwoman would whisper even in the intimacy of her own thoughts was exceptional. The type remains, and in many ways it is a pathetic one—timid, immature, and so uneducated that it never doubts its ability to order the lives of its betters.

But there is no hope of arguing with people of that kind, for they are not mature enough to understand discussion. Even in countries like England and France with an old and educated middle class the censorship of literature has never resulted in anything except absurdity. How could it be otherwise? Law requires a strict definition of terms and no one has ever been able to define obscenity. No attempt at definition has stood up to the test of experience. Nowadays the idea of prosecuting the authors of *Madame Bovary* and *Fleurs du Mal,* which are part of every Frenchman's education, seems ludicrous, but it happened, and prosecutions still go on.

Except for a certain criminal element, not entirely unknown even on the bench, and which is, or should be, a matter for the criminal courts, the question of decency in literature is not one of morals but of manners. Morals concern themselves with what is right and wrong, manners with what is suitable and unsuitable. Obscenity is occasionally not only a social duty but a pleasure—a great Englishman laid it down that it is the only sort of conversation which pleases both sexes—and it is merely a question of when and where we are permitted to indulge in it and the only judge of that is society itself. If you've ever attended a dinner party with a pathological teller of indecent stories as I have you realise what Hell opened to sinners is like, but you don't ring for the police.

That is why the disease of censorship does not thrive among the aristocracy or among peasants. Living a natural life, as they both do, they don't confuse morals and manners, and besides both have a rigorous code of manners. None of her kinsmen thought the worse of the great Countess of Argyll for having written an Irish poem to her chaplain's—manners forbid my mentioning what—and her poem has been preserved for us by the piety of a scholarly Dean. Censors are nearly always townsmen, unfamiliar with nature and with no traditional code of manners that would permit them to discuss their own animal nature without embarrassment and guilt.

A much more entertaining book than *Lady Chatterley's Lover* is *The Trial of Lady Chatterley,* the report of the law case, for here, because of the fact that nobody can produce a legal definition of obscenity, we see a number of learned and famous people behaving like characters in a low farce. On the one hand we have a Prosecutor and a Judge who seem to believe quite sincerely that four-letter words and descriptions of sexual union are in themselves indecent and degrading. On the other we have a lot of high-minded people, including an Anglican bishop, who seem to believe that, on the contrary, they are desirable and even elevating. Nobody connected with the case seems to have even suspected that they are neither. So far as *Lady Chatterley's Lover* is concerned, they are merely unmannerly, grossly unmannerly. No mannerly society, aristocratic or peasant, could have produced such an uncouth book.

But of course you can't prosecute a book merely for being unmannerly, so the prosecution is compelled to base its case on an imaginary injury to an imaginary individual, and the defence is driven to suggesting an imaginary benefit to some equally imaginary individual. The result was the immediate sale of two million copies of the book, a result that I don't think the prosecution desired. I doubt if even the Bishop of Woolwich desired it. But this is what comes of calling in the police in a question that involves manners. Our only safeguard against pathological indecency is in the instinct which we all share to protect the memory of our own parents as we hope our children will protect ours, the instinct Shakespeare speaks of when he makes a character say:

> I have been harsh
> To large confessors, and have hotly asked them
> If they had mothers? I had one, a woman,
> And women 'twere they wronged.

But however absurd it may have been, the trial of *Lady Chatterley's Lover* was an honest attempt by serious people to define what they meant by evil literature. No one in his senses could pretend that this has ever been the aim of the Irish Censorship. To begin with, it is a sort of dual-purpose institution, a double-barrelled shotgun pointing in different directions, so that if it doesn't get the duck it may get the rabbit. It proscribes indecent literature, but it also proscribes any favourable reference to birth control. Anything I might say to you on that subject could not be printed in Ireland. If it were, Mr. Justice Conroy and his colleagues would be bound to suppress it and Mr. Justice Haugh and his colleagues would be bound to support their decision.[2] That is not a censorship of indecent literature, that is a censorship of opinion and a censorship exercised on behalf of one creed. It is class legislation because it militates against the working class while the well-to-do Catholics and the pale primrose Protestants make their own arrangements. What these are we can only guess—a close study of the work of Dr. Halliday Sutherland or something more practical?[3]

But the conjunction is revealing of the type of mind behind the censorship, because, as you will remember, Dr. Halliday Sutherland's work was also banned, and during the extraordinary Senate debate on censorship the Minister for Justice defended the ban by saying that Dr. Sutherland's book was "the fornicator's vade mecum." I have a suspicion that the then Minister for Justice had little experience of fornicators if he thought them normally addicted to the higher mathematics. But that is by the way. What really counts is the attitude of mind, the determination to get at sex by hook or by crook. Sex is bad, books encourage sex, babies deter it, so keep the books out and give them lots of babies, and we shall have the nearest thing the Puritan can hope for to a world without beauty and romance.

That is why I regret that Mr. Justice Conroy and Mr. Justice Haugh are now presiding over those two absurd boards. I know that they have done their work honestly and well. I should know it from the character of Judge Haugh even if I did not know it from the test they will not permit to be applied to the books they censor—the test of public approval. I am sure that the greatest scandal which attached to the work of their predecessors—that of the deliberate suppression of every serious book by an Irish writer—has been considerably abated, though it should never have existed at all, and that I and other writers are indebted to them for a more sympathetic attention than we should otherwise have received. Unfortunately, I don't want to depend for protection on any individual, whatever his taste and judgment. As a citizen of this country I want to depend for protection on the constitution and the courts. Anything less than that is outlawry. And, as I have said before, when there was no pretence of law the censorship represented the reality of the situation with which I as a writer must deal—the bookless homes, the horrible libraries, each with its own little group of censors, sniffing out sex that the Censorship Board had failed to detect, the customs officials who try to give the censors a helping hand by seizing books by every author whose name they know and keeping them for months until they are no longer saleable.

This is the reality for which two High Court judges are the facade, and in many ways it is as dangerous and inhuman as the pathological indecency of Apollinaire and Sade. Among the treasure documents of one Irish public library were two letters, both written by the same man, a respected public figure. The first letter was a complaint to the librarian and committee that among the books in the library was an indecent work called *Tom Jones* by an Englishman, Henry Fielding. The second letter, written a few weeks later, was a reply to a complaint that he had accosted a girl in the lending library. He assured the committee, of course, that he hadn't intended to accost her at all, merely to point out to her an interesting passage in a book he was looking at. There is a more than casual affinity between the pathological censor and the pathological pornographer. It is almost symbolic that the first work by a major writer to be banned by the Irish Censorship Board was Liam O'Flaherty's *The Puritan*. That, I fancy, hit too close to home.

But to me the most awful thing about the censorship is the way it perpetuates the negative attitude we oppose to every manifestation of intellect and scholarship. We can find no better employment for two brilliant judges of our High Court than a task that could be adequately performed by a policeman with a bit of intelligence. We have a Censorship Board and a Censorship Appeal Board, but we have no such thing as a Society for the Encouragement of Irish Literature, over which Mr. Justice Haugh or Mr. Justice Conroy might preside with honour to himself and benefit to his country. We have a Censorship Board, but we have no publishers. We have a great literature, published by Englishmen and Americans, and, thanks to our censors, ninety-nine per cent of it is out of print and unobtainable, so that, as I have said before, we have brought up a generation which knows nothing of its own country, or its own literature. Be as moral as you please, have all the censorships you think necessary, but be positive about it. Don't merely ban books, publish them. If we can't read the filthy works of J. D. Salinger like *The Catcher in the Rye* or *For Esme with Love and Squalor* is there any reason why we can't put back into print the hundreds of books by Irish writers which are essential to our very survival as a literate people—books like Carleton's *Autobiography, The Tailor and Ansty, The Irish Countryman,* and *Reminiscences of a Maynooth Professor?*

> You have the Pyrrhic dance as yet,
>   Where is the Pyrrhic phalanx gone?
> Of two such lessons, why forget
>   The nobler and the manlier one?
> —*Byron,* Don Juan, *III, lxxxvi, 10*

In conclusion, think of that one book, *The Tailor and Ansty* and consider its history. In this country it was banned as indecent and obscene. Only one public man defended it—Sir John Keane, who wasn't either pale or primrose, and in replying to him in the Senate one of our national heroes described the Tailor as "a dirty old man" and his wife as "a moron."[4] As a result that kind old couple who had offered their simple hospitality to students from all over Ireland were boycotted. I am not exaggerating. I was there with them one night when a branch of a tree was driven between the wall and the latch so that we were imprisoned. Three priests appeared at their little cottage one day and forced that dying old man to go on his knees at his own hearth and burn the only copy he had of his own book.

When Mr. Justice Haugh took over the Censorship Appeal Board he and his colleagues discovered to nobody's astonishment that *The Tailor and Ansty* was not obscene at all. But by that time, of course, the Tailor and Ansty were dead and the book out of print. It is still out of print. But the statue of the Tailor as one of the Apostles stands over a Catholic Church in San Francisco, and *The Tailor and Ansty* has been taught in Harvard University by an American anthropologist. Must we always depend on foreigners to teach us the difference between a pornographic book and a masterpiece? Have we no independent scholarship or criticism? What a race of humbugs we are!

I am asked to propose to you that the Irish censorship is an insult to Irish intelligence. Gentlemen of the Jury, if you feel otherwise I can only say that Irish intelligence is a contradiction in terms.

Notes

Introduction

1. Michael Adams, *Censorship: The Irish Experience* (Dublin: Scepter Books, 1968), 13–15. This study is the principal source for information on censorship of publications in Ireland. For general information on social and cultural history of the period see Terence Brown, *Ireland: A Social and Cultural History, 1922–1985* (London: Fontana, 1987).

2. For detailed discussion of these events see W. B. Yeats, *Dramatis Personae, 1896–1902* (New York: Macmillan, 1936), 34; James Kilroy, *The "Playboy" Riots* (Dublin: Dolmen Press, 1971); and Alan Simpson, *Beckett and Behan and a Theatre in Dublin* (London: Routledge and Kegan Paul, 1962), 138–67.

3. Censorship of Publications Act, 1929 (Dublin: Stationery Office, 1929).

4. Adams, *Censorship*, 21–24.

5. Ibid., 46, 207.

6. Quoted in Kieran Woodman, *Media Control in Ireland, 1923–1983* (Galway: Officina Typographica, 1985), 50.

7. Quoted in Adams, *Censorship*, 49.

8. Ibid., 46.

9. W. B. Yeats, *The Letters of W. B. Yeats*, ed. Allan Wade (London: Rupert Hart-Davis, 1954), 801–2.

10. Mervyn Wall, interview with Julia Carlson, Dublin, 6 October 1987. Unless otherwise indicated, all further quotations from Mervyn Wall are taken from this interview.

11. Quoted in Brown, *Ireland*, 146.

12. Quoted in Woodman, *Media Control in Ireland*, 33–34.

13. Adams, *Censorship*, 37.

14. Mervyn Wall, letter to Julia Carlson, 11 May 1989.

15. Mervyn Wall, interview with Julia Carlson.

16. Adams, *Censorship,* 47, 66, 72–73.

17. Kate O'Brien, *The Land of Spices* (Garden City, N.Y.: Doubleday, Doran and Co., 1941), 175.

18. Adams, *Censorship,* 85, 213.

19. For a discussion of censorship and Irish booksellers see L. M. Cullen, *Eason and Son: A History* (Dublin: Eason, 1989).

20. Dermot Foley, "A Minstrel Boy with a Satchel of Books," *Irish University Review* 4 (Autumn 1974): 211.

21. Dermot Foley, interview with Julia Carlson, Dublin, 30 October 1987. All further quotations from Dermot Foley are taken from this interview.

22. Mervyn Wall, interview with Julia Carlson.

23. Adams, *Censorship,* 84.

24. Sean O'Faolain, "Our Nasty Novelists," *Bell* 2 (August 1941): 12.

25. Frank O'Connor, "The Stone Dolls," *Bell* 2 (June 1941): 65–67.

26. Dermot Foley, interview with Julia Carlson.

27. This judgement was made in favour of the Society for the Protection of the Unborn Child (SPUC) in the High Court on 19 December 1986 and was upheld in the Supreme Court on 16 March 1988.

Interviews

Benedict Kiely

1. Ironically, James Joyce's *Ulysses* was never banned in Ireland, even though it was banned in both Britain and the United States.

2. Eilis Dillon, "Sean O'Faolain and the Young Writer," *Irish University Review* 6 (Spring 1976): 41.

3. The *Irish Press* was founded by Eamon de Valera in 1931 as the newspaper of the Fianna Fail party.

4. Benedict Kiely, "The Whores on the Half-Doors; or an Image of the Irish Writer," in *Conor Cruise O'Brien Introduces Ireland,* ed. Owen Dudley Edwards (London: Andre Deutsch, 1969), 151.

5. Ibid., 152.

6. In 1982 Aosdana was founded to recognize achievement in the arts; artists who are members are eligible to apply for a yearly annuity. All writers are eligible to apply to the Arts Council for bursaries, and since 1969 earnings from published works have been tax-free for approved writers.

7. Two crucial referendums were held in Ireland in the 1980s. When the Referendum (Amendment) Act, 1983, was passed, it became impossible for abortion to be legalized in Ireland by any government working under the present constitution. In 1986 a bill to introduce divorce into Ireland was defeated in a referendum by a substantial majority.

8. Kiely, "The Whores on the Half-Doors," 158.

John Broderick

1. The Eucharistic Congress was a week-long celebration held in Dublin in June of 1932. Church dignitaries and pilgrims, including the papal legate, came from all over the world. Special buildings and trains were provided, and candlelit Masses were held throughout the week in the Phoenix Park. At one service over a million people were present. As symbolic as it was religious, the congress celebrated Ireland's new identity as a Catholic nation, revealing the influence that the Catholic church would have in the future life of the country.

2. See Rev. Peter R. Connolly, "Censorship," *Christus Rex* 13 (1959): 151–70. In this landmark article, Connolly called for a reassessment of the Irish censorship policy, arguing that Ireland "should not be bereft of the salutary criticism of some of its own most passionately aware members," and warned that the continued censorship of the bulk of modern literature would lead only to further "cynicism about the Act and contempt for Censorship in general." Connolly also spoke against Irish censorship at public meetings, including one in Limerick in 1966 where he defended Edna O'Brien's work. For a description of this meeting see Sean McMahon, "A Sex by Themselves: An Interim Report on the Novels of Edna O'Brien," *Eire-Ireland* 2 (1967): 80.

3. Ireland is bound by the European Convention on Human Rights, which it signed in 1953. Irish citizens may complain of human rights violations to the European Commission on Human Rights.

John McGahern

1. The Irish National Schools, established under British rule to offer free primary education to Irish children, are state-supported but church-controlled.

2. Throughout the 1950s Owen Sheehy Skeffington campaigned actively against censorship in the Irish Senate. He gave strong support to John McGahern in "McGahern Affair," *Censorship* 2 (Spring 1966): 27–30.

3. The Irish amateur dramatic movement began to play a major role in the social and cultural life of rural Ireland in the late 1930s. While the movement brought a cultural life to isolated areas, it remained essentially conservative in its approach to the arts. It is still active today, and its annual festivals are highly popular.

4. In the right-to-life debates that preceded the Abortion Referendum in 1983, pressure groups such as the Society for the Protection of the Unborn Child and the Pro-Life Amendment Campaign campaigned vigorously in favour of the pro-life amendment to the constitution.

5. Under section 31 of the 1960 Broadcasting Authority Act, Radio Telefís Eireann is prohibited from broadcasting interviews with members of subversive organizations—with spokesmen for the Irish Republican Army, for organizations classed as unlawful in Northern Ireland, and for Provisional Sinn Fein. Article 19 is currently supporting a legal challenge of this ban before the European Commission of Human Rights in Strasbourg.

Edna O'Brien

1. See, for example, Bruce Arnold, "Censorship and Edna O'Brien," *Irish Times,* 21 November 1966. Benedict Kiely comments on "the current determined persecution of the novels of Edna O'Brien" in "The Whores on the Half-Doors," 158–60.

2. Grace Eckley, *Edna O'Brien* (Lewisburg: Bucknell University Press, 1974), 26.

3. Bolivar Le Franc, "Committed to Mythology," *Books and Bookmen* 13 (September 1968): 53.

4. Le Franc, "Committed to Mythology," 53.

Lee Dunne

1. Members of the Censorship Board are appointed by the minister for justice. The Censorship of Publications Act does not require that the board be representative of a cross-section of the population or that representatives of publishers' or writers' groups serve on the board.

2. For evidence of this prejudice see Adams, *Censorship,* 45. It also is clear in the wording of the Censorship of Publications Act, which states that consideration is to be given to "the class of reader . . . which may reasonably be expected to read such a book or edition" (pt. II, sec. 6).

Brian Moore

1. Eoin MacNeill was chief of staff of the Irish Volunteers during the Easter Rising of 1916 and became the Irish Free State's first minister of education. He was professor of early Irish history at University College, Dublin, and was known for his work in the Gaelic League.

2. Anne Haverty, "The Outsider on the Edge," *Sunday Tribune,* 3 November 1985.

Appendix

All notes in the appendix have been supplied by the editor.

[Russell], The Censorship Bill

1. It was originally proposed that "recognised associations," such as the Catholic Truth Society, be authorized to bring material to the attention of the Censorship Board. This suggestion was rejected, however, and responsibility for submitting material to the Censorship Board was put in the hands of customs officials and the public at large.

Yeats, The Censorship and St. Thomas Aquinas

1. Professor W. F. Trench, who held the chair of English literature at Trinity College, wrote in favour of censorship in 1928; later he protested against it, attacking the Censorship Board for banning Sean O'Faolain's *Bird Alone* in 1936.

Shaw, The Censorship

1. Dublin Castle was the centre of British administration in Ireland.

2. The British home secretary, Sir William Joynson Hicks, supported the passage of the Judicial Proceedings (Regulations of Reports) Act, 1926, and in 1928 threatened to tighten controls on obscene publications. He later advocated censorship in his pamphlet, "Do We Need a Censor?" (1929).

O'Flaherty, The Irish Censorship

1. For a description of the Eucharistic Congress see n. 1 to the Broderick interview.

Beckett, Censorship in the Saorstat

1. This article is highly topical in its references, and Beckett refers to places in Dublin such as the Tate and Brady restaurant and draws in detail from both the Censorship of Publications Act, 1929, and the debates in the Irish Parliament that led up to the passage of the act.

2. Marie Stopes and Margaret Sanger were among the first authors to have their books banned by the Censorship Board.

O'Connor, Frank O'Connor on Censorship

1. Mr. Justice Kevin Haugh was appointed chairman of the first Appeal Board in 1946 and served until 1968.

2. Mr. Justice J. C. Conroy was appointed chairman of the Censorship Board in 1957 and served until 1975.

3. Dr. Halliday Sutherland's *Laws of Life,* which advocated natural birth control, was banned by the Irish Censorship Board in 1942 and became the subject of a heated debate in the Irish Senate in November and Decem-

ber of that year. Two other banned books were also debated at that time, Kate O'Brien's novel *The Land of Spices,* and *The Tailor and Ansty* by Eric Cross.

4. Sir John Keane opposed the 1929 Censorship of Publications Act, and in the 1942 Senate debates on censorship he repeatedly condemned actions taken by the Censorship Board.

Select Bibliography

Adams, Michael. *Censorship: The Irish Experience*. Dublin: Scepter Books, 1968.

Barrington, Margaret, Hubert Butler, L. Huban, and Monk Gibbon. "Public Opinion: Censorship." *Bell* 9 (March 1945): 528–35.

Blanshard, Paul. *The Irish and Catholic Power: An American Interpretation*. London: Verschoyle, 1954.

Bristow, Ann. "Dublin's Book Banners." *Index on Censorship* 10 (April 1981): 28–31.

Broderick, John. "The Labelling of Lee Dunne." *Hibernia*, 11 May 1973, 21.

Brown, Terence. *Ireland: A Social and Cultural History, 1922–1985*. London: Fontana, 1987.

Connolly, Rev. Peter R. "Censorship." *Christus Rex* 13 (1959): 151–70.

Foley, Dermot. "A Minstrel Boy with a Satchel of Books." *Irish University Review* 4 (Autumn 1974): 204–17.

———. "Monotonously Rings the Little Bell." *Irish University Review* 6 (Spring 1976): 54–62.

Foster, John Wilson. *Forces and Themes in Ulster Fiction*. Dublin: Gill and Macmillan, 1974.

Gibbon, Monk. "In Defence of Censorship." *Bell* 9 (January 1945): 313–21.

Hackett, Francis. "A Muzzle Made in Ireland." *Dublin Magazine* 11, n.s. 4 (1936): 8–17.

Kavanagh, Patrick. "The Wake of the Books." *Bell* 15 (November 1947): 4–16.

Kiely, Benedict. *Modern Irish Fiction: A Critique*. Dublin: Eagle Books, 1950.

————. "The Whores on the Half-Doors; or an Image of the Irish Writer." In *Conor Cruise O'Brien Introduces Ireland,* edited by Owen Dudley Edwards. London: Andre Deutsch, 1969.

Lyster, M. "Padraic Colum on the Censorship." *Irish Statesman* 11 (1928): 107–8.

MacManus, Francis. "The Literature of the Period." In *The Years of the Great Test, 1926–39,* edited by Francis MacManus. Cork: Mercier Press, 1967.

O'Connor, Frank. Introduction to *The Tailor and Ansty,* by Eric Cross. New York: Devin-Adair Company, 1964.

[O'Donnell, Peadar.] "Taking Stock." *Bell* 18 (January 1953): 453–55.

[O'Faolain, Sean.] "Books and a Live People." *Bell* 6 (May 1943): 91–98.

O'Faolain, Sean. "The Dangers of Censorship." *Ireland Today* 1 (December 1936): 57–63.

[————.] "1916–1941: Tradition and Creation." *Bell* 2 (April 1941): 5–12.

[————.] "Our Nasty Novelists." *Bell* 2 (August 1941): 5–12.

[————.] "The Senate and Censorship." *Bell* 5 (January 1943): 247–52.

[————.] "Standards and Taste." *Bell* 2 (June 1941): 5–11.

[————.] "The State and Its Writers." *Bell* 7 (November 1943): 93–99.

Russell, George [AE, pseud.] "The Censorship in Ireland." *Nation and Athenaeum,* 22 December 1928, 435–36.

———— [Y.O., pseud.] "Literature and Life: Passions and Principles." *Irish Statesman* 11 (1928): 30–31.

St. John-Stevas, Norman. *Obscenity and the Law.* London: Secker and Warburg, 1956.

Shaw, Bernard. Preface to *The Shewing-up of Blanco Posnet.* In *Prefaces by Bernard Shaw.* London: Odhams Press, 1938.

Shaw, G. Bernard, Sean O'Casey, T. C. Kingsmill Moore, and Professor James Hogan. "Censorship: Comments by Readers." *Bell* 9 (February 1945): 395–409.

Skeffington, Owen Sheehy. "McGahern Affair." *Censorship* 2 (Spring 1966): 27–30.

Smith, Edward Doyle. *A Survey and Index of the* Irish Statesman *(1923–1930)*. Ann Arbor, Mich.: University Microfilms, 1966.

Wall, Mervyn. "An Address." *Journal of Irish Literature* 11 (January–May 1982): 63–79.

Woodman, Kieran. *Media Control in Ireland, 1923–1983*. Galway: Officina Typographica, 1985.

Yeats, W. B. "The Irish Censorship." *Spectator,* 29 September 1928, 391–92. Reprinted in W. B. Yeats, *The Senate Speeches of W. B. Yeats,* edited by Donald R. Pearce. London: Faber and Faber, 1961. Also reprinted in W. B. Yeats, *Uncollected Prose.* Vol. 2, *Reviews, Articles and Other Miscellaneous Prose, 1897–1939,* edited by John P. Frayne and Colton Johnson. London: Macmillan, 1975.

Index